Testimonials and Comments
for the ElderCare Ready Book and the ElderCare Ready Pack

"Stuart Furman is an exceptional and technically skilled attorney and his clients greatly benefit from his bountiful real life experiences. Stuart's approach with the *ElderCare Ready Pack*, and its sister publication the *ElderCare Ready Book*, couples his legal savvy with his practical advice providing the reader with the confidence to navigate the very challenging waters of eldercare."

Pete Potente, Esq.
Potente Law, PC

"As my characters Earl and Opal have discovered, growing older has its ups and downs. My comics have always been about the funny side of growing older, but the less humorous side of aging can be difficult for families to handle. *The ElderCare Ready Book* is a valuable tool to help families brace for the challenges ahead and get through the difficulties of aging by becoming more organized and prepared."

Brian Crane,
Creator of the Pickles comic strip

"*The ElderCare Ready Book* is a valuable resource for those taking care of an elderly family member. Mr. Furman hit the nail on the head when writing this book. When the caregiver is in the workforce, using *The ElderCare Ready Book* to be organized and prepared for their caregiving voyage will help reduce productivity loss for the employee, human resources department, and company owners."

Natasha Sandrock Arthur, PHR-CA, CCP, GRP
Director, Human Resources
CaVU Consulting, Inc.
President of San Diego Society for
Human Resource Management (2013–2014)

The ElderCare
READY PACK

STUART FURMAN

Eldercare Ready, LLC
555 Country Club Lane, Suite C-315
Escondido, California 92026
legal@eldercareready.com
www.eldercareready.com

Ordering Information:
Quantity sales: Special discounts are available on quantity purchases by corporations, associations, and others. For details, contact the author at the address above.
Orders by US trade bookstores and wholesalers:
Please contact Eldercare Ready, LLC.
Tel: (toll-free) 800-551-7505
Fax: (760) 749-2926
e-mail: orders@eldercareready.com
or visit us at: www.eldercareready.com

Published by ElderCare Ready, LLC
555 Country Club Lane, Suite C-315
Escondido, California 92026, USA
www.eldercareready.com

ISBN: 978-0-9905292-2-4
LCCN: 2015904678

Dedication & Thanks

Dedicated to:
Seymour Furman, my dad;
Marion Furman, my mom;
Miriam Bender, my wife's mother;
Charles Evans, my wife's father; and
Eugene Bender, my mother-in-law's second husband,
all of whom provided the inspiration for this book.

Special thanks to
my wife, Jayne, and
Cara Ouellette, my legal assistant,
for their valuable insight and assistance.

Very special thanks to:
Brian Crane,
creator of the Pickles comic strip,
for his comment and permitted use of his comic strips in this book.

Protection of Sensitive Information

Many items contained herein ask for you to list passwords, account numbers, and other access information codes. Please take great care to protect this book from theft or viewing by unauthorized persons. You may wish to list sensitive information in another location, provided that the information is readily available to you when needed. The author makes no representation as to what information is considered sensitive and is left to the judgement of the reader.

CONTENTS

What is the *ElderCare Ready Book* and Why Should You Read it First?

The *ElderCare Ready Book* (let's call it the "Book") is really the preface to this *ElderCare Ready Pack*. In the Book I explain how the concept for the Book and *ElderCare Ready Pack* (from now on, the "Pack") was born and why it has become such a valuable tool for those on their eldercare journey. In the Book, you will read my story and how my wife and I struggled with taking care of several parents. This is important to give the reader context and to describe how events unfolded in our lives. I suspect those of you on your eldercare journey will find similarities to our stories.

In particular, I discuss in the Book what eldercare really is and when is the right time to start your eldercare journey. There is a description of information and documentation that you will need and why you will need it. A very important section is titled "releases" which describes how to gain access to information when you need it. This release chapter also describes the different types of documents that you will run into, including living trusts, and the various types of powers of attorney. Read this chapter in the Book as it is vitally important to assure you that you have access to your loved one's information and documentation under another's control. The Book continues with the importance of conducting a safety check and security check, what to expect from care providers, a description of types of care facilities and a glossary of terms that you will run into. Finally I had to add a chapter on "Famous Last Words" which describes the top things that clients have told me and have done that have cost them dearly. This section may be able to help you avoid these problems too.

This *ElderCare Ready Pack* is the implementation of the concepts described in the Book. It is a fill-in-the-blanks handbook for the information and documentation that you will need on your eldercare journey.

Why not have an online or electronic version of the *ElderCare Ready Pack*?

In this day and age where electronics dominate most of our daily lives, why create a hard copy version of this handbook rather than an electronic version or website to contain all of this information? This is actually quite simple. First, it is no secret that many of the major data-bases have been, and are continuing to be, hacked and very sensitive information is stolen. This creates a truly frightening data security crisis. Having control of the information where it cannot be seen by anyone except the person in possession of this Pack is vital to keep information secure. The only proviso is that you cannot lose it. Guard it religiously. Second, and perhaps more importantly, the information and documentation you will accumulate with the guidance of this Pack need to be readily and immediately available by you or others that are caring for your loved one. You probably would not want to give your computer to someone else and provide them with your security password to access this information (for example, your sibling may need to take mom to the doctor), or have to login to a website to be able to email documents or information over the Internet. Think about this scenario. You are at the emergency room and the doctor needs the medication list. With your laptop, you need to boot up your computer, connect to a website, get the email where it is to be sent, send it, print out a copy and deliver it to the doctor. Most emergency rooms also do not have an email that they want to give out to the public. This Pack will contain the information and it can be immediately communicated to the doctor. There will also be times where there is no service, your device is out of battery life, the Internet is down, or other situations where electronics actually hinder your ability to make quick and good decisions.

I learned early on in my eldercare journey that a crisis will happen between Friday night and Sunday night and usually in the middle of the night. The Pack is a self-contained package that explains what documentation and information that you will need so all you need to do is get in the car and go.

Why This *ElderCare Ready Pack* is So Important

As described in the Book, the need for families to assist in the caregiving of the older generation is on the rise, along with its attendant stresses, strains, frustrations, and time commitments. The cared-for senior also feels uneasiness and guilt, as well as the same frustrations, stresses, and strains due to slowly losing control of independence, affairs, and health. The common goal here is to bridge the gap between generations so that the aging process can be more comfortable, controllable, and understandable.

This *ElderCare Ready Pack* is like a suitcase. You pack everything you will need for your journey so you are prepared to make decisions when they need to be made. Your information library is with you and easily accessible.

Who Will Provide Eldercare?

Our definition of family has changed. There are many more second or third marriages. There are "yours, mine, and ours" families when referring to children. Many family members care for their stepparent as if he or she were their own. This was the case with my mother-in-law and her second husband after she was widowed. I have seen the younger generations taking care of aunts and uncles, brothers and sisters, and other distant relatives and friends. So for purposes of this Pack, I refer to the older generations as the "elder" or "elders," but keep in mind that this definition can apply to the above relationships or to others.

Who is This Pack For?

This Pack is for people who are providing eldercare to an elder and for the elders who are being cared for. It is intended to assist in helping to care for an elder with their full consent, cooperation, and knowledge. This Pack is not intended to be a resource for anyone to access another person's information without his or her consent. Consent must be established either through discussion with the elder while they are mentally competent, or via previously established communication and agreement, such as by the elder executing a power of attorney, living trust, or other legal documentation, giving appropriate authority for a person to act on their behalf. Above all, it is vital to protect the wellbeing of the elder, including their financial and personal privacy, to the greatest extent possible. Ideally, this book and other eldercare publications should be used for you to work together with the elder to prepare for future issues and events. The information in this Pack should never be used to take advantage of an elderly person, to act on the elder's behalf without authority, or to utilize the elder's information in a way that may compromise his or her personal, financial, and legal privacy and security.

This Pack may also be for YOU to organize all of YOUR affairs in one compact place in anticipation of you needing care.

What is This Pack About?

Again, this Pack is the implementation of having, immediately at hand, the organized, complete, and necessary information and documentation to manage your elder's health and other affairs when the elder is unable to do so on his or her own. The Pack prompts you as to the relevant information and documentation that you will need for your eldercare journey as described in the Book.

Although your elder's care needs will continually vary, this Pack prepares you for whatever divergence they will take. Countless events can happen, and it is impossible to direct someone as to all the situations that arise. Therefore it is vitally important to be prepared in advance for the decisions that await you. This Pack is the tool to deal with the foreseeable and unforeseeable events that you will experience on your journey.

This Pack also contains a glossary of certain terms, in addition to the glossary in the Book, that you will come across and a description of the types of care provided by independent care providers that you will run into.

When you first flip through the sections in this Pack, it appears a bit ominous. But the more you review the sections that apply to your eldercare journey, the more you will realize that the information is actually very readily available. It just has to be consolidated into one useful location....the *ElderCare Ready Pack*. The more complete the information, the more prepared you are for your journey. You may think that certain sections are not that important to be completed. That may be so...or not! I have found that "Murphy's Law" always applies: the information I don't have at the moment is exactly what I need. I have provided the means for a successful journey, but only you can actually take the trip. I hope this Pack will help dissipate some of your anxiety through preparation. It did for me.

* * * *

Chapter 1

THE ELDERCARE READY SYSTEM

The ElderCare Ready System

AFTER ROUGHLY TWENTY YEARS OF having practiced elder law and estate planning, my wife and I seemed to have been caught totally off-guard when we realized that our parents had gotten old. Their health started to fail, each in their own way, mentally or physically.

I began the practice of law in December of 1981, not knowing exactly in what area of law I was going to practice. After beginning my career, I immediately realized that the "knowledge" of law that I learned in law school was far different from the "practice" and the "business" of law in the real world. Similarly, advising and consulting with clients about their loved ones was completely different than having to deal with day-to-day eldercare issues. Once I had to do what my client families had to do regularly, it was a real eye-opener for me. It was like starting over in a completely different field. I describe in detail what this eldercare role is in my *ElderCare Ready Book*, but simply it is the management of your elder's care and wellbeing. It includes managing their finances, taxes, arranging doctor appointments and taking them to those appointments, visiting, calling and checking up on them, handling emergencies and trips to the hospital that, believe me, will happen, and much more.

Because of my knowledge of the law and then my experience in providing eldercare, I realized that the vast majority of families do not have the luxury of understanding both sides of the equation. So I created the *ElderCare Ready System* to prepare the reader for his or her own eldercare journey. This system does not make the critical decisions that affect your elder's life as those have to be made in the moment with the options presented to you. It does however assist you in preparing for those decisions by prompting you as to the information that you will need in an organized manner.

The *ElderCare Ready System* is a unique approach to managing your eldercare journey. There are three prongs to this system. First is the *ElderCare Ready Book* which gives the reader background and context as to your eldercare journey. It also explains in clear text format what documentation and information you will need to pack on your eldercare travels. Finally it acts as the preface for the *ElderCare Ready Pack*. The *ElderCare Ready Pack* is a fill-in-the-blanks implementation of the concepts relayed in the *ElderCare Ready Book*. Finally the *ElderCare Ready Journal* at www.eldercareready.com keeps you up to date on eldercare related issues, news stories, helpful tips and additional needed information or documentation that become evident due to the changes in the world. The Journal will routinely disseminate inserts, and replacement pages, for the *ElderCare Ready Pack* when needed to keep your Pack complete and current.

My mantra is and will always be: "Don't fear eldercare, just be prepared for it". Your eldercare role will be thrust upon you. It will occur to some extent so just pack your eldercare suitcase and get ready to travel with just about everything that you need.

* * * *

Chapter 2

RELEASES

ONE OF THE MOST FRUSTRATING parts of managing the care of an elder is not having access to necessary information when you need it. Again, how many times have you called a company, such as a bank or brokerage company, or a professional, like an attorney or doctor, or anyone else on behalf of another person, and the response is "I cannot give you any information because you are not authorized," or "you are not on the account, so I cannot give you any information"? You need access to information. Knowledge is the key to the eldercare lockbox.

This is an ongoing and evolving problem. Although this chapter is a bit complex, I hope that the following discussion will help alleviate some of your confusion, not increase it, and provide some guidance about how to gain access to your elder's financial, personal, and medical information when needed. If you become frustrated, remember that although it may not give you much comfort, you are certainly not alone!

Throughout this book, you may have seen references to having a "release." I am using this as a very general term, which is intended to mean that the appropriate and necessary document required by the individual or institution (as outlined in this chapter) has been provided and accepted as sufficient to gain access to the elder's information and documentation.

What is Access Exactly?

Access to information is different from having the ability to sign on the accounts and transact business. Often you may just want information about a bank account balance, a check that cleared, or a credit card charge, but are not looking to sign for the elder or make a transaction. The document required to gain access to the information can often be different from the document needed to have the ability to sign on an account, and a power of attorney is not always better than a release or consent to release information. Unfortunately, institutions (banks, brokerage firms, credit card companies, service companies, etc.) and professionals (doctors, lawyers, accountants, etc.) each have their own rules and policies.

Keep in mind that a power of attorney is signed to give someone the power and authority to act for the person creating the power of attorney, and the authority to have access to information. The sole purpose of a release is to give someone access to information and documentation but not to take action on behalf of the person signing the release.

Ownership Type and Living Trusts

Gaining access to the elder's individually held asset information (such as bank transaction history or account balance history) is accomplished quite differently than gaining access to asset information where the asset is held in a living trust. Simply put, a power of attorney generally has no relevance when asking someone to give information about an asset held in a living trust. It is like comparing apples to oranges. So if you go to the bank with a power of attorney and ask for a balance for an account held in a living trust, the bank will refuse your request.

Generally, access to financial information in a revocable living trust requires a release signed by the trustee (who is typically the elder) in his or her capacity as trustee of the trust. The release has to say something like this: *"I, Jim Roe, trustee of the Jim Roe Living Trust, hereby consent to the release of any and all information…"* If the trustee is not the elder but is another person acting as trustee for the elder's living trust, the acting trustee would issue the release. So the release would say something like this: *"I, Jane Doe, trustee of the Jim Roe Living Trust, hereby consent to the release of any and all information…"* Again, a power of attorney is generally inadequate in this situation, as the elder executed the power of attorney in his or her individual capacity rather than in his or her capacity as trustee. The account held in the trust is not the same as the account of the individual. This gets a bit confusing, but here is an example to help clarify this.

John Smith is a customer at ABC Bank. John has three accounts with ABC Bank:

Account 1: A checking account that the bank shows is owned by John Smith.

Account 2: A checking account that the bank shows is owned by John Smith, trustee of the John Smith Living Trust.

Account 3: An individual retirement account (IRA) that the bank shows is owned by John Smith.

If John's daughter Nancy (for example) wanted to have access to and make transactions on John's accounts, what sort of document might she use to accomplish this?

Account 1: This account is owned by John alone. No other person is listed as an owner on the account. Nancy would use a power of attorney to access the account, if John's power of attorney lists her as the agent who can act on his behalf and the power of attorney gives Nancy the requisite authority to do banking for John.

Account 2: This account is not owned by John individually, even though it is owned by

John's own living trust. Therefore, Nancy would not be able to use a power of attorney to access this account. Nancy would need the authority (through a legal document) to be able to act for John's trust. If John is still competent to sign documents, this may be accomplished by amending the John Smith Living Trust and adding Nancy as cotrustee. If John was not competent to sign documents and if she were listed as a successor trustee to John, a showing of John's incompetency perhaps by medical certifications of incapacity will legally secure her as the acting trustee of John's trust. She then has access to the accounts in John's living trust.

Account 3: Like account 1, account 3 is owned by John Smith individually (not in a trust), so Nancy might be able to use the power of attorney to transact on this account.

Remember that each state has different laws regarding legal documents and each bank, institution, or other entity may have their own rules regarding accessing account information and making transactions, so the above examples may not hold true in every situation.

Also, joint tenancy (such as an account that has two people as account holders), IRA, and 401(k) assets, for example, are not assets of a living trust. Some assets like life insurance may be in the living trust. So it is important to determine how ownership of each of the assets is held to provide the proper releases.

Powers of Attorney (POA)

Some of this is counterintuitive and confusing. This section will also clearly point out why to not just download a power of attorney off the Internet or buy one from the local office supply store. Contrary to folklore, powers of attorney are not all the same and must be reviewed very carefully. Only an attorney should prepare a power of attorney for the elder after consultation as to the type of power of attorney that best fits the elder's personal circumstances.

If a power of attorney is being presented to access the elder's information, make sure that the power of attorney is currently effective. That sounds weird doesn't it? Why sign a power of attorney that is not effective? Determining the type of power of attorney will affect how you access the necessary information and how and when you can act for the elder.

A currently effective power of attorney (POA) is where a person (the "principal") gives another person (the "agent" or "attorney-in-fact") the power to act for the principal. A power of attorney without durable provisions, described below, will terminate upon death or incompetency (legal incapacity) of the principal.

A currently effective durable power of attorney (DPOA) states that the principal is currently granting the authority to the agent (the person who is named to take action for the grantor of the power of attorney). The authority stays in effect after the principal (the one granting the power of attorney) has become legally incapacitated. This is called "durable" language, and without it, as described above, the power of attorney will terminate upon the legal incapacity of the elder. Please see the chapter called Famous Last Words relating to powers of attorney.

Another widely used type of power of attorney is a springing durable power of attorney (SDPOA). This refers to a durable power of attorney that becomes effective only after the principal (the one granting the power of attorney) has become legally incapacitated (this is also durable language). The power of attorney "springs" into effect upon legal incapacity. Many clients only want the power of attorney to be used if they have become incompetent. They may not want to give up control until it is necessary, so this type of POA fits their purposes. Additionally, the definition of incapacity (as used in each particular power of attorney) will be defined within the power of attorney document itself. For example, the springing power of attorney might state that two medical doctors have to certify that the principal is incapacitated in order for the authority under the power of attorney to spring into effect. You cannot use this type of power of attorney until the power has "sprung." It is like a power of attorney in waiting.

You must also look to the authority granted in the POA, DPOA, or SDPOA. Powers of attorney that do not grant all authority to the agent are called limited or special powers of attorney. You may not have been granted the particular authority that you are trying to act upon or use, so the appropriate authority needs to be identified in the document. Additionally, even if the POA, DPOA, or SDPOA states that it gives all possible powers that the principal has to the agent, there are still powers that may not be granted as they are controlled by state statute and must be expressly stated in the document. For example, California law says that the power to gift the principal's assets or to create a trust on behalf of the principal must be specifically drafted ("expressly stated," in legal terms) in the document or it still does not exist.[1] Again, this is even if the power of attorney states that the agent is granted all conceivable authority, whether listed or not listed.

A frustrating aspect of gaining access to information or using powers of attorney is aging, regardless of the type of power of attorney being presented. Many financial institutions will not accept a power of attorney if it is too old, even though by definition in California law, for example, it is still valid and in full force and effect![2] "Too old" is defined by the policies of each institution. I have had clients where the company refused to accept a power of attorney that was only six months old, so be sure to check with the institution beforehand. You can easily see a real conundrum when the elder has a "springing" durable power of attorney (one that comes into effect when the elder is no longer competent), and when the elder is later deemed to be legally incapacitated and thus can no longer execute legal documents, the bank says the power of attorney is too old!

Also, many institutions, especially banks, often do not accept powers of attorney other than

---

1   Per California Probate Code § 4264.
2   Per California Probate Code § 4127.

on their own forms, so you may need to get pushy with the institution to accept the power of attorney that you submit. This has been a frustration for attorneys and families across the country.

Medical Information

Medical records and information are usually accessed using a HIPAA release which is a release of medical information, similar to how a financial release works. This document is signed by the elder, granting a release of medical records and information to the named individuals. Be careful, as a HIPAA form signed at the elder's physician's office may not name you as an authorized party, and you may think you have a valid HIPAA release giving you access to the elder's medical records when you actually do not.

A power of attorney for health care, often called an "advance medical directive" or similar document in your state, may also provide access to medical information but is typically designed to grant you authority to make decisions for the elder if the elder cannot make such decisions on his or her own.

Legal/Attorney Matters

Attorneys will need a release of some sort before disclosing a client's information to any third party. There is a privileged relationship between the elder and his or her attorney (other such relationships exist between doctors and patients and with the clergy, for example). So the confidentiality must be released, or waived, in writing, before the attorney will disclose any information, whether orally or in writing. The release could be signed by an agent under the elder's power of attorney if the power or attorney grants the agent the authority to do so.

Other Professionals

CPAs, financial planners, and other professionals do not enjoy the same legally privileged relationships but often will require a release or consent to allow their information to be disseminated to another person. Similarly, a power of attorney may also be sufficient.

Banks and Financial Institutions

Financial account information held in the elder's name only will generally require a power of attorney or consent to release information to gain access to the financial data.

Safe deposit boxes will generally require your name on the signature card to gain access. Banks often will not accept any type of power of attorney to access the box of the elder. They also do not know what is in the box, so access is the only way to discover what is in there.

Premade Forms and Releases

Forms downloaded from the Internet may not provide the authority that you need in all situations that you will come across. Tragically, in these cases, you may not be able to have new documents signed by the elder due to his or her incapacity when you are informed that the submitted document is insufficient. If a person is determined to be legally incapacitated (such as when their doctor certifies that they do not have the mental capacity to understand the nature of their personal matters), he or she will no longer be able to sign legal documents (such as a power of attorney, living trust, or last will). In my practice, I have found the Internet documents woefully inadequate in the vast majority of cases. I strongly recommend having an estate planning attorney draft appropriate documents for the elder's particular situation.

What to Do

To ensure that the proper releases or consents are delivered to all the people and companies holding information or documents that you may need along your eldercare journey, contact each one and ask what documents they will accept to grant access. Then, deliver that document to them and confirm that it is effective to grant you access to information, now and in the future. If you are seeking to change the signing authority on an account or asset or to add yourself as a signer, take the same action and ensure that you will be able to transact all necessary business on behalf of your elder when the time comes for you to step in and assist.

If the elder does not yet want you to be able to sign on his or her account, and if the elder is mentally competent, have the power of attorney, living trust, and other estate planning documents reviewed by an estate planning attorney so when the elder is no longer legally competent, you can access the information needed and transact business for the elder. This way, if the document is insufficient for your needs, the elder can execute a replacement document while he or she is still competent to do so.

* * * *

Notes:

_____

_____

_____

_____

_____

_____

_____

_____

_____

_____

_____

_____

_____

_____

_____

_____

_____

_____

_____

_____

_____

_____

_____

_____

_____

_____

_____

_____

_____

Notes:

Notes:

Chapter 3

PERSONAL INFORMATION

My Story:

"The Costo experience is always fun. All three parents need adult diapers. It is really fun to see the looks from everyone when you are carting three boxes (Costco size boxes) of adult diapers around Costco. They look at you. They look at the boxes to see if they are men's or women's diapers. You know they are trying to figure out how old you are and when they might need to walk the diaper gauntlet of embarrassment themselves."

Personal Information

Personal information about the elder is vital for several reasons. Some of the following material provides security words and codes to access accounts and other financial information. If an elder wanders off (and you have heard stories about this on the news) a description of the elder can make the difference between finding that person or not. Details about implants, medical devices, and physical limitations assist first responders and other medical personnel when trying to help the elder.

Full Legal Name _____

                      [First]   [Middle]   [Last]

AKA/Other Names _____

                      [First]   [Middle]   [Last]

_____

                      [First]   [Middle]   [Last]

Nickname _____

Phone Numbers   Home _____

                    Cell   _____

                    Fax   _____

Mailing Address _____

_____

Physical Address _____

_____

Email Addresses _____

_____

Gender   [ ] Male   [ ] Female
Social Security Number (SSN)   _____ – _____ – _____
Date of Birth   _____/_____/_____
Mother's Maiden Name   _____
Place of Birth (City, State, Country)   _____,_____,_____
Driver's License/State Identification   State _____, Number_____, Exp_____
Passport Information   Country _____, Number_____, Exp_____
Does this person have a conservator or a guardian?   Yes _____   No _____
If so, Case Number _____, County/State of Court _____
Name of Conservator/Guardian _____, of the [ ] Person or [ ] Estate
Is this person a veteran?   Yes _____   No _____
        Date of Entry   _____/_____/_____
        Exit Date   _____/_____/_____
        Service Branch   _____   Rank _____
        Service Number   _____
        Discharge Type   [ ] Honorable   [ ] General [ ] Dishonorable
Personal Information
        Height   _____   Weight   _____
        Hair Color   _____   Eye Color   _____
        Blood Type   _____   Religion   _____
Languages (check all that apply)
        [ ]   English   [ ] Spanish   [ ] _____
        [ ]   _____   [ ] _____   [ ] _____
        [ ]   _____   [ ] _____   [ ] _____
Medical Implants/Devices (check all that apply)
        [ ]   Pacemaker
               Maker _____, Model # _____, Serial # _____
        [ ]   Stent (Location _____)
               Maker _____, Model # _____, Serial # _____
        [ ]   Stent (Location _____)
               Maker _____, Model # _____, Serial # _____
        [ ]   Stent (Location _____)
               Maker _____, Model # _____, Serial # _____
        [ ]   Hip Replacement (Left)
               Maker _____, Model # _____, Serial # _____
        [ ]   Hip Replacement (Right)
               Maker _____, Model # _____, Serial # _____

[ ]   Knee Replacement (Left)

    Maker _____, Model # _____, Serial # _____

[ ]   Knee Replacement (Right)

    Maker _____, Model # _____, Serial # _____

[ ]   Shoulder Replacement (Left)

    Maker _____, Model # _____, Serial # _____

[ ]   Shoulder Replacement (Right)

    Maker _____, Model # _____, Serial # _____

[ ]   Implanted Port (Port-a-Cath)

    Maker _____, Model # _____, Serial # _____

[ ]   Other Replacement/Prosthetic (Item/Location _____)

    Maker _____, Model # _____, Serial # _____

[ ]   Other Replacement/Prosthetic (Item/Location _____)

    Maker _____, Model # _____, Serial # _____

[ ]   Other Replacement/Prosthetic (Item/Location _____)

    Maker _____, Model # _____, Serial # _____

[ ]   Other Replacement/Prosthetic (Item/Location _____)

    Maker _____, Model # _____, Serial # _____

Medical Equipment/Devices (check all that apply)

[ ]	Dentures	[ ]	Braces	[ ]	Glasses
[ ]	Cane	[ ]	Walker	[ ]	Reading Glasses

[ ]   Walker

    Maker _____, Color _____

[ ]   Hearing Aids

    Maker _____, Model # _____, Serial # _____

[ ]   Wheelchair

    Maker _____, Model # _____, Serial # _____

[ ]   Cart/Electric Scooter/Chair

    Maker _____, Model # _____, Serial # _____

[ ]   Colostomy Bag

    Maker _____, Model # _____, Serial # _____

[ ]   Oxygen

    Maker _____, Model # _____, Serial # _____

[ ]   Urinary Catheter

    Maker _____, Model # _____, Serial # _____

[ ]   Other Medical Equipment/Device (Item _____)

    Maker _____, Model # _____, Serial # _____

[ ]   Other Medical Equipment/Device (Item _____)
         Maker _____, Model # _____, Serial # _____
[ ]   Other Medical Equipment/Device (Item _____)
         Maker _____, Model # _____, Serial # _____
[ ]   Other Medical Equipment/Device (Item _____)
         Maker _____, Model # _____, Serial # _____

Physical Limitations

[ ]   Non-Ambulatory   [ ]   Needs Assistance w/Eating
[ ]   Bowel Incontinent   [ ]   Needs Assistance w/Bathing
[ ]   Bladder Incontinent   [ ]   Needs Assistance w/Dressing
[ ]   Hard of Hearing   [ ]   Needs Assistance w/Grooming
[ ]   Blind   [ ]   Deaf
[ ]   Other _____   [ ]   Other _____
[ ]   Other _____   [ ]   Other _____
[ ]   Other _____   [ ]   Other _____

Most Recent Spouse	
Full Legal Name	_____
Date of Marriage	_____/_____/_____
Is this person deceased?	Yes _____ No _____ Date of Death _____
Is this spouse divorced?	Yes _____ No _____ Divorce Date _____
Gender	[ ] Male [ ] Female
Social Security Number (SSN)	_____–____–_____
Date of Birth	_____/_____/_____
Mother's Maiden Name	_____
Phone Numbers Home	_____
Cell	_____
Address	_____
	_____
Email Address	_____
Place of Birth (City, State, Country)	_____,_____,_____
Driver's License/State Identification	State _____, Number_____, Exp_____
Passport Information	Country_____, Number_____, Exp_____
Is this person a veteran?	Yes _____ No _____

Previous Spouse

Full Legal Name _____

Date of Marriage _____/_____/_____

Is this person deceased? Yes _____ No _____ Date of Death _____

Is this spouse divorced? Yes _____ No _____ Divorce Date _____

Gender [ ] Male [ ] Female

Social Security Number (SSN) _____ – _____ – _____

Date of Birth _____/_____/_____

Mother's Maiden Name _____

Phone Numbers Home _____

Cell _____

Address _____

_____

Email Address _____

Place of Birth (City, State, Country) _____,_____,_____

Driver's License/State Identification State _____, Number_____, Exp_____

Passport Information Country_____, Number_____, Exp_____

Is this person a veteran? Yes _____ No _____

Previous Spouse

Full Legal Name _____

Date of Marriage _____/_____/_____

Is this person deceased? Yes _____ No _____ Date of Death _____

Is this spouse divorced? Yes _____ No _____ Divorce Date _____

Gender [ ] Male [ ] Female

Social Security Number (SSN) _____ – _____ – _____

Date of Birth _____/_____/_____

Mother's Maiden Name _____

Phone Numbers Home _____

Cell _____

Address _____

_____

Email Address _____

Place of Birth (City, State, Country) _____,_____,_____

Driver's License/State Identification State _____, Number_____, Exp_____

Passport Information Country_____, Number_____, Exp_____

Is this person a veteran? Yes _____ No _____

Notes:

_____

_____

_____

_____

_____

_____

_____

_____

_____

_____

_____

_____

_____

_____

_____

_____

_____

_____

_____

_____

_____

_____

_____

_____

_____

_____

_____

_____

Notes:

Chapter 4

CONTACTS

My Story:

"My dad needed an ambulance trip to the ER after a fall. Nothing was broken, but he still couldn't walk for a few days, so we needed to arrange for a non-medical transport to return him to his assisted living community, while still being transported on a stretcher. We followed him home and as he was being removed from the van on the stretcher (all strapped in), he said "thanks…that was a really nice trip and I had a wonderful time!" Sometimes they say the darndest things!"

Family & Friends

1)   Name _____   Phone Number _____

      Relationship _____   Cell Number _____

      Address _____

      Email(s) _____

2)   Name _____   Phone Number _____

      Relationship _____   Cell Number _____

      Address _____

      Email(s) _____

3)   Name _____   Phone Number _____

      Relationship _____   Cell Number _____

      Address _____

      Email(s) _____

4)   Name _____   Phone Number _____

      Relationship _____   Cell Number _____

      Address _____

      Email(s) _____

5)   Name _____   Phone Number _____

      Relationship _____   Cell Number _____

      Address _____

      Email(s) _____

6) Name _____ Phone Number _____

    Relationship _____ Cell Number _____

    Address _____

    Email(s) _____

7) Name _____ Phone Number _____

    Relationship _____ Cell Number _____

    Address _____

    Email(s) _____

8) Name _____ Phone Number _____

    Relationship _____ Cell Number _____

    Address _____

    Email(s) _____

9) Name _____ Phone Number _____

    Relationship _____ Cell Number _____

    Address _____

    Email(s) _____

10) Name _____ Phone Number _____

    Relationship _____ Cell Number _____

    Address _____

    Email(s) _____

11) Name _____ Phone Number _____

    Relationship _____ Cell Number _____

    Address _____

    Email(s) _____

12) Name _____ Phone Number _____

    Relationship _____ Cell Number _____

    Address _____

    Email(s) _____

13) Name _____ Phone Number _____

    Relationship _____ Cell Number _____

    Address _____

    Email(s) _____

Medical Professionals

Physician (list primary physician first)

  Name _____ Specialty _____

  Address _____

  Phone Number _____ Fax Number _____

  Email(s) _____

  [ ] Release on File

Other Physician

  Name _____ Specialty _____

  Address _____

  Phone Number _____ Fax Number _____

  Email(s) _____

  [ ] Release on File

Other Physician

  Name _____ Specialty _____

  Address _____

  Phone Number _____ Fax Number _____

  Email(s) _____

  [ ] Release on File

Other Physician

  Name _____ Specialty _____

  Address _____

  Phone Number _____ Fax Number _____

  Email(s) _____

  [ ] Release on File

Other Physician

  Name _____ Specialty _____

  Address _____

  Phone Number _____ Fax Number _____

  Email(s) _____

  [ ] Release on File

Other Physician
    Name _____ Specialty _____
    Address _____
    Phone Number _____ Fax Number _____
    Email(s) _____
    [ ] Release on File

Pharmacy
    Name _____
    Address _____
    Phone Number _____ Fax Number _____
    Email(s) _____
    [ ] Release on File

Pharmacy
    Name _____
    Address _____
    Phone Number _____ Fax Number _____
    Email(s) _____
    [ ] Release on File

Dentist
    Name _____
    Address _____
    Phone Number _____ Fax Number _____
    Email(s) _____
    [ ] Release on File

Podiatrist
    Name _____
    Address _____
    Phone Number _____ Fax Number _____
    Email(s) _____
    [ ] Release on File

Chiropractor

    Name _____

    Address _____

    Phone Number _____ Fax Number _____

    Email(s) _____

    [ ] Release on File

Physical Therapist

    Name _____

    Address _____

    Phone Number _____ Fax Number _____

    Email(s) _____

    [ ] Release on File

Geriatric Care Manager

    Name _____

    Address _____

    Phone Number _____ Fax Number _____

    Email(s) _____

    [ ] Release on File

Other Medical Professional

    Name _____ Specialty _____

    Address _____

    Phone Number _____ Fax Number _____

    Email(s) _____

    [ ] Release on File

Other Medical Professional

    Name _____ Specialty _____

    Address _____

    Phone Number _____ Fax Number _____

    Email(s) _____

    [ ] Release on File

Legal & Financial Professionals

Attorney (Main)
    Name _____ Specialty _____
    Address _____
    Phone Number _____ Fax Number _____
    Email(s) _____
    [ ] Release on File

Other Attorney
    Name _____ Specialty _____
    Address _____
    Phone Number _____ Fax Number _____
    Email(s) _____
    [ ] Release on File

Other Attorney
    Name _____ Specialty _____
    Address _____
    Phone Number _____ Fax Number _____
    Email(s) _____
    [ ] Release on File

Conservatorship/Guardianship Attorney
    Name _____
    Address _____
    Phone Number _____ Fax Number _____
    Email(s) _____
    [ ] Release on File

CPA/Accountant
    Name _____
    Address _____
    Phone Number _____ Fax Number _____
    Email(s) _____
    [ ] Release on File

Financial Professional/Advisor

    Name _____

    Address _____

    Phone Number _____ Fax Number _____

    Email(s) _____

    [ ] Release on File

Conservator/Guardian

    Name _____ Conservator of   [ ] Person   [ ] Estate

    Address _____

    Phone Number _____ Fax Number _____

    Email(s) _____

    [ ] Release on File

Other Financial Professional/Advisor

    Name _____

    Address _____

    Phone Number _____ Fax Number _____

    Email(s) _____

    [ ] Release on File

Other Financial Professional/Advisor

    Name _____

    Address _____

    Phone Number _____ Fax Number _____

    Email(s) _____

    [ ] Release on File

Other Financial Professional/Advisor

    Name _____

    Address _____

    Phone Number _____ Fax Number _____

    Email(s) _____

    [ ] Release on File

Insurance Agents

Health Insurance Agent

    Name _____

    Address _____

    Phone Number _____ Fax Number _____

    Email(s) _____

    [ ] Release on File

Homeowners Insurance Agent

    Name _____

    Address _____

    Phone Number _____ Fax Number _____

    Email(s) _____

    [ ] Release on File

Renters Insurance Agent

    Name _____

    Address _____

    Phone Number _____ Fax Number _____

    Email(s) _____

    [ ] Release on File

Long Term Care Insurance (LTCI) Agent

    Name _____

    Address _____

    Phone Number _____ Fax Number _____

    Email(s) _____

    [ ] Release on File

Disability Insurance Agent

    Name _____

    Address _____

    Phone Number _____ Fax Number _____

    Email(s) _____

    [ ] Release on File

Auto Insurance Agent

    Name _____

    Address _____

    Phone Number _____ Fax Number _____

    Email(s) _____

    [ ] Release on File

Burial Insurance/Prepaid Funeral Plan Agent

    Name _____

    Address _____

    Phone Number _____ Fax Number _____

    Email(s) _____

    [ ] Release on File

Life Insurance Agent

    Name _____

    Address _____

    Phone Number _____ Fax Number _____

    Email(s) _____

    [ ] Release on File

Life Insurance Agent

    Name _____

    Address _____

    Phone Number _____ Fax Number _____

    Email(s) _____

    [ ] Release on File

Annuity Agent

    Name _____

    Address _____

    Phone Number _____ Fax Number _____

    Email(s) _____

    [ ] Release on File

Annuity Agent
    Name _____
    Address _____
    Phone Number _____ Fax Number _____
    Email(s) _____
    [ ] Release on File

Other Agent
    Name _____ Specialty _____
    Address _____
    Phone Number _____ Fax Number _____
    Email(s) _____
    [ ] Release on File

Other Agent
    Name _____ Specialty _____
    Address _____
    Phone Number _____ Fax Number _____
    Email(s) _____
    [ ] Release on File

Other Agent
    Name _____ Specialty _____
    Address _____
    Phone Number _____ Fax Number _____
    Email(s) _____
    [ ] Release on File

Other Agent
    Name _____ Specialty _____
    Address _____
    Phone Number _____ Fax Number _____
    Email(s) _____
    [ ] Release on File

Senior Placement Agencies

Senior Placement Agency/Company
　　Name _____
　　Address _____
　　Phone Number _____ Fax Number _____
　　Email(s) _____
　　[ ] Release on File

Senior Placement Agency/Company
　　Name _____
　　Address _____
　　Phone Number _____ Fax Number _____
　　Email(s) _____
　　[ ] Release on File

Clergy & Funeral Preparations

Church/Religious Representative
　　Name _____ Religion _____
　　Address _____
　　Phone Number _____ Fax Number _____
　　Email(s) _____
　　Name of Church/Organization _____
　　[ ] Release on File

Funeral Director/Home
　　Name _____
　　Address _____
　　Phone Number _____ Fax Number _____
　　Email(s) _____
　　Type of Service Requested (Cremation/Burial/etc.) _____
　　Disposition of Remains Requested (urn, scattering of ashes, etc.) _____
　　_____
　　Other Instructions _____
　　_____
　　[ ] Release on File

Other Contact Person

    Name _____ Relationship _____

    Address _____

    Phone Number _____ Fax Number _____

    Email(s) _____

    [ ] Release on File

Other Contact Person

    Name _____ Relationship _____

    Address _____

    Phone Number _____ Fax Number _____

    Email(s) _____

    [ ] Release on File

Desired Guest List for Funeral/Burial Service

Name _____ Relationship _____

Name _____ Relationship _____

Name _____ Relationship _____

Name _____ Relationship _____

Name _____ Relationship _____

Name _____ Relationship _____

Name _____ Relationship _____

Name _____ Relationship _____

Name _____ Relationship _____

Name _____ Relationship _____

Name _____ Relationship _____

Name _____ Relationship _____

Name _____ Relationship _____

Name _____ Relationship _____

Name _____ Relationship _____

Name _____ Relationship _____

Name _____ Relationship _____

Name _____ Relationship _____

Name _____ Relationship _____

Name _____ Relationship _____

Notes:

_____

_____

_____

_____

_____

_____

_____

_____

_____

_____

_____

_____

_____

_____

_____

_____

_____

_____

_____

_____

_____

_____

_____

_____

_____

_____

_____

_____

_____

_____

_____

Notes:

_____

_____

_____

_____

_____

_____

_____

_____

_____

_____

_____

_____

_____

_____

_____

_____

_____

_____

_____

_____

_____

_____

_____

_____

_____

_____

_____

_____

_____

_____

_____

Notes:

_____

_____

_____

_____

_____

_____

_____

_____

_____

_____

_____

_____

_____

_____

_____

_____

_____

_____

_____

_____

_____

_____

_____

_____

_____

_____

_____

_____

_____

_____

_____

_____

Chapter 5

MEDICAL INFORMATION

My Story:

"Hospital trips are loads of fun, especially when you are not prepared for the information that the hospital will need. On my dad's first visit to the ER, the personnel rightfully wanted to know what medications he was taking. We didn't really know so we called the assisted living facility where he was living, and after tracking someone down to handle the matter, they gave the med list to the ER nurse. You would think that was all they needed after they entered the information into their computer. WRONG! The doctor came in to see my dad and guess what his first question was? Right…what meds is he taking? Again, I had no clue, since I didn't write them down but rather had just given my phone to the nurse, so we had to call the assisted living facility again. After my dad was admitted to the hospital later that day, the first question that the nurse asked was "What medications is he taking?" The doctor comes in again to see my dad, and believe it or not, he asks "What medications is he taking?" I was shocked and perplexed, especially since each person had entered the information into the computer each time I was asked. Always have a current med list that you can just give to all appropriate parties."

Health Insurance & Coverage

Medicare

    Policy Number _____

    Prescription (Rx) Policy Number _____

HMO/PPO

    Company Name _____

    Address _____

    Phone Number _____

    Policy Number/ID _____

Other HMO/PPO

    Company Name _____

    Address _____

    Phone Number _____

    Policy Number/ID _____

Medicaid/Medi-Cal/State Health Insurance

    Program Name _____

    Address _____

    Phone Number _____

    Policy Number/ID _____

Other Government Insurance/SSDI

    Program Name _____

    Address _____

    Phone Number _____

    Policy Number/ID _____

Prescription Drug Supplement

    Company Name _____

    Address _____

    Phone Number _____

    Plan Name _____

    Policy Number/ID _____

Long Term Care Insurance (LTCI)

    Company Name _____

    Address _____

    Phone Number _____

    Plan Name _____

    Policy Number/ID _____

    Description of Coverage _____

    _____

Other Policy

    Company Name _____

    Address _____

    Phone Number _____

    Plan Name _____

    Policy Number/ID _____

    Member ID _____

    Group Number _____

    Plan Code _____

    Payor ID _____

    Description of Coverage _____

    _____

    _____

Other Policy

    Company Name _____

    Address _____

    Phone Number _____

    Plan Name _____

    Policy Number/ID _____

    Member ID _____

    Group Number _____

    Plan Code _____

    Payor ID _____

    Description of Coverage _____

    _____

Other Policy

    Company Name _____

    Address _____

    Phone Number _____

    Plan Name _____

    Policy Number/ID _____

    Member ID _____

    Group Number _____

    Plan Code _____

    Payor ID _____

    Description of Coverage _____

    _____

* * * *

Health History & Miscellaneous Information

Vaccination History

    Type of Vaccination _____

                Administered on date   _____/_____/_____

    Type of Vaccination _____

                Administered on date   _____/_____/_____

    Type of Vaccination _____

                Administered on date   _____/_____/_____

    Type of Vaccination _____

                Administered on date   _____/_____/_____

    Type of Vaccination _____

                Administered on date   _____/_____/_____

    Type of Vaccination _____

                Administered on date   _____/_____/_____

    Type of Vaccination _____

                Administered on date   _____/_____/_____

    Type of Vaccination _____

                Administered on date   _____/_____/_____

    Type of Vaccination _____

                Administered on date   _____/_____/_____

Medical History - Prior Injuries

    Type of Injury   _____

                Occurred on date   _____/_____/_____

    Type of Injury   _____

                Occurred on date   _____/_____/_____

    Type of Injury   _____

                Occurred on date   _____/_____/_____

    Type of Injury   _____

                Occurred on date   _____/_____/_____

    Type of Injury   _____

                Occurred on date   _____/_____/_____

    Type of Injury   _____

                Occurred on date   _____/_____/_____

    Type of Injury   _____

                Occurred on date   _____/_____/_____

Medical History - Prior Injuries (continued)

Type of Injury _____

Occurred on date _____/_____/_____

Type of Injury _____

Occurred on date _____/_____/_____

Type of Injury _____

Occurred on date _____/_____/_____

Medical History - Prior Surgeries

Type of Surgery _____

Date of procedure _____/_____/_____
Name of physician _____

Type of Surgery _____

Date of procedure _____/_____/_____
Name of physician _____

Type of Surgery _____

Date of procedure _____/_____/_____
Name of physician _____

Type of Surgery _____

Date of procedure _____/_____/_____
Name of physician _____

Type of Surgery _____

Date of procedure _____/_____/_____
Name of physician _____

Type of Surgery _____

Date of procedure _____/_____/_____
Name of physician _____

Type of Surgery _____

Date of procedure _____/_____/_____
Name of physician _____

Organ Donation

Does this person desire to donate their organs upon death?   [ ] yes   [ ] no

If so, for what purposes? (check all that apply)

[ ] transplant   [ ] research   [ ] therapy   [ ] education

Donation registered with the state/correct agency?   [ ] yes   [ ] no

Medical & Mental Conditions

Current Mental/Cognitive Status (check all that apply)

[ ] Legally incapacitated (certification of medical doctor or court order)

[ ] Dementia

[ ] Alzheimer's Disease

[ ] Mild cognitive impairment

[ ] Competent

[ ] Not sure

[ ] Other _____

Medical and Mental Conditions/Diagnoses (fill in as needed)

[ ] _____

[ ] _____

[ ] _____

[ ] _____

[ ] _____

[ ] _____

[ ] _____

[ ] _____

[ ] _____

[ ] _____

[ ] _____

[ ] _____

[ ] _____

[ ] _____

[ ] _____

[ ] _____

Allergies (fill in type of allergy)

[ ] _____

[ ] _____

[ ] _____

[ ] _____

[ ] _____

[ ] _____

[ ] _____

[ ] _____

Medication List Instructions

It is suggested that you post a copy of the Quick Reference Current Medication List in the residence or room of the elder. This is for the first responders and medical professionals to be able to immediately know which medications the elder is taking. Please do be aware, however, that privacy may be a concern if your elder lives in a community setting, so while this list should be easily accessible for medical and emergency professionals, you may want to keep it out of plain sight to preserve their privacy.

The Quick Reference Current Medication List should include both recurring and regular medications that the elder is taking. This needs to be updated as medications are started or terminated.

The Detailed and Recurring Medication List is for those medicines that are being prescribed to be taken on a regular basis to manage a specific illness or condition. For example, a statin drug used to manage high cholesterol that is taken every evening would be a recurring medication. However, an antibiotic that is taken to manage a one-time infection would not be a "recurring medication" in most cases.

The Detailed and Non-recurring Medication List is for those medicines that are being prescribed to be taken on a periodic or temporary basis to manage a short-term illness or condition (like the antibiotic example mentioned above).

These detailed lists are more inclusive so they can be helpful with periodic reordering of the drugs and other maintenance, so the physician name, pharmacy information, prescription number can be listed for ease of reordering and management.

* * * *

Quick Reference Current Medication List

- Rx Name _____ Dosage _____
  How often taken? _____ Discontinued? [ ]
- Rx Name _____ Dosage _____
  How often taken? _____ Discontinued? [ ]
- Rx Name _____ Dosage _____
  How often taken? _____ Discontinued? [ ]
- Rx Name _____ Dosage _____
  How often taken? _____ Discontinued? [ ]
- Rx Name _____ Dosage _____
  How often taken? _____ Discontinued? [ ]
- Rx Name _____ Dosage _____
  How often taken? _____ Discontinued? [ ]
- Rx Name _____ Dosage _____
  How often taken? _____ Discontinued? [ ]
- Rx Name _____ Dosage _____
  How often taken? _____ Discontinued? [ ]
- Rx Name _____ Dosage _____
  How often taken? _____ Discontinued? [ ]
- Rx Name _____ Dosage _____
  How often taken? _____ Discontinued? [ ]
- Rx Name _____ Dosage _____
  How often taken? _____ Discontinued? [ ]
- Rx Name _____ Dosage _____
  How often taken? _____ Discontinued? [ ]
- Rx Name _____ Dosage _____
  How often taken? _____ Discontinued? [ ]
- Rx Name _____ Dosage _____
  How often taken? _____ Discontinued? [ ]
- Rx Name _____ Dosage _____
  How often taken? _____ Discontinued? [ ]
- Rx Name _____ Dosage _____
  How often taken? _____ Discontinued? [ ]
- Rx Name _____ Dosage _____
  How often taken? _____ Discontinued? [ ]
- Rx Name _____ Dosage _____
  How often taken? _____ Discontinued? [ ]

Detailed Regular & Recurring Medication List

- Rx Name _____ Dosage _____
  How often taken? _____
  Dates taken, from _____/_____/_____ to _____/_____/_____
  Prescribing Physician _____
  Prescribing Physician Phone Number _____
  Prescribed for this Condition _____
  Pharmacy/Pharmacist Name _____
  Phone Number _____ Prescription Number _____

- Rx Name _____ Dosage _____
  How often taken? _____
  Dates taken, from _____/_____/_____ to _____/_____/_____
  Prescribing Physician _____
  Prescribing Physician Phone Number _____
  Prescribed for this Condition _____
  Pharmacy/Pharmacist Name _____
  Phone Number _____ Prescription Number _____

- Rx Name _____ Dosage _____
  How often taken? _____
  Dates taken, from _____/_____/_____ to _____/_____/_____
  Prescribing Physician _____
  Prescribing Physician Phone Number _____
  Prescribed for this Condition _____
  Pharmacy/Pharmacist Name _____
  Phone Number _____ Prescription Number _____

- Rx Name _____ Dosage _____
  How often taken? _____
  Dates taken, from _____/_____/_____ to _____/_____/_____
  Prescribing Physician _____
  Prescribing Physician Phone Number _____
  Prescribed for this Condition _____
  Pharmacy/Pharmacist Name _____
  Phone Number _____ Prescription Number _____

- Rx Name _____ Dosage _____
  How often taken? _____
  Dates taken, from   _____/_____/_____   to   _____/_____/_____
  Prescribing Physician _____
  Prescribing Physician Phone Number _____
  Prescribed for this Condition _____
  Pharmacy/Pharmacist Name _____
  Phone Number _____   Prescription Number _____

- Rx Name _____ Dosage _____
  How often taken? _____
  Dates taken, from   _____/_____/_____   to   _____/_____/_____
  Prescribing Physician _____
  Prescribing Physician Phone Number _____
  Prescribed for this Condition _____
  Pharmacy/Pharmacist Name _____
  Phone Number _____   Prescription Number _____

- Rx Name _____ Dosage _____
  How often taken? _____
  Dates taken, from   _____/_____/_____   to   _____/_____/_____
  Prescribing Physician _____
  Prescribing Physician Phone Number _____
  Prescribed for this Condition _____
  Pharmacy/Pharmacist Name _____
  Phone Number _____   Prescription Number _____

- Rx Name _____ Dosage _____
  How often taken? _____
  Dates taken, from   _____/_____/_____   to   _____/_____/_____
  Prescribing Physician _____
  Prescribing Physician Phone Number _____
  Prescribed for this Condition _____
  Pharmacy/Pharmacist Name _____
  Phone Number _____   Prescription Number _____

- Rx Name _____ Dosage _____
  How often taken? _____
  Dates taken, from _____/_____/_____ to _____/_____/_____
  Prescribing Physician _____
  Prescribing Physician Phone Number _____
  Prescribed for this Condition _____
  Pharmacy/Pharmacist Name _____
  Phone Number _____ Prescription Number _____

- Rx Name _____ Dosage _____
  How often taken? _____
  Dates taken, from _____/_____/_____ to _____/_____/_____
  Prescribing Physician _____
  Prescribing Physician Phone Number _____
  Prescribed for this Condition _____
  Pharmacy/Pharmacist Name _____
  Phone Number _____ Prescription Number _____

- Rx Name _____ Dosage _____
  How often taken? _____
  Dates taken, from _____/_____/_____ to _____/_____/_____
  Prescribing Physician _____
  Prescribing Physician Phone Number _____
  Prescribed for this Condition _____
  Pharmacy/Pharmacist Name _____
  Phone Number _____ Prescription Number _____

- Rx Name _____ Dosage _____
  How often taken? _____
  Dates taken, from _____/_____/_____ to _____/_____/_____
  Prescribing Physician _____
  Prescribing Physician Phone Number _____
  Prescribed for this Condition _____
  Pharmacy/Pharmacist Name _____
  Phone Number _____ Prescription Number _____

- Rx Name _____ Dosage _____
  How often taken? _____
  Dates taken, from _____/_____/_____   to   _____/_____/_____
  Prescribing Physician _____
  Prescribing Physician Phone Number _____
  Prescribed for this Condition _____
  Pharmacy/Pharmacist Name _____
  Phone Number _____ Prescription Number _____

- Rx Name _____ Dosage _____
  How often taken? _____
  Dates taken, from _____/_____/_____   to   _____/_____/_____
  Prescribing Physician _____
  Prescribing Physician Phone Number _____
  Prescribed for this Condition _____
  Pharmacy/Pharmacist Name _____
  Phone Number _____ Prescription Number _____

- Rx Name _____ Dosage _____
  How often taken? _____
  Dates taken, from _____/_____/_____   to   _____/_____/_____
  Prescribing Physician _____
  Prescribing Physician Phone Number _____
  Prescribed for this Condition _____
  Pharmacy/Pharmacist Name _____
  Phone Number _____ Prescription Number _____

- Rx Name _____ Dosage _____
  How often taken? _____
  Dates taken, from _____/_____/_____   to   _____/_____/_____
  Prescribing Physician _____
  Prescribing Physician Phone Number _____
  Prescribed for this Condition _____
  Pharmacy/Pharmacist Name _____
  Phone Number _____ Prescription Number _____

- Rx Name _____ Dosage _____
  How often taken? _____
  Dates taken, from _____/_____/_____ to _____/_____/_____
  Prescribing Physician _____
  Prescribing Physician Phone Number _____
  Prescribed for this Condition _____
  Pharmacy/Pharmacist Name _____
  Phone Number _____ Prescription Number _____

- Rx Name _____ Dosage _____
  How often taken? _____
  Dates taken, from _____/_____/_____ to _____/_____/_____
  Prescribing Physician _____
  Prescribing Physician Phone Number _____
  Prescribed for this Condition _____
  Pharmacy/Pharmacist Name _____
  Phone Number _____ Prescription Number _____

- Rx Name _____ Dosage _____
  How often taken? _____
  Dates taken, from _____/_____/_____ to _____/_____/_____
  Prescribing Physician _____
  Prescribing Physician Phone Number _____
  Prescribed for this Condition _____
  Pharmacy/Pharmacist Name _____
  Phone Number _____ Prescription Number _____

- Rx Name _____ Dosage _____
  How often taken? _____
  Dates taken, from _____/_____/_____ to _____/_____/_____
  Prescribing Physician _____
  Prescribing Physician Phone Number _____
  Prescribed for this Condition _____
  Pharmacy/Pharmacist Name _____
  Phone Number _____ Prescription Number _____

- Rx Name _____ Dosage _____
  How often taken? _____
  Dates taken, from _____/_____/_____   to _____/_____/_____
  Prescribing Physician _____
  Prescribing Physician Phone Number _____
  Prescribed for this Condition _____
  Pharmacy/Pharmacist Name _____
  Phone Number _____   Prescription Number _____

- Rx Name _____ Dosage _____
  How often taken? _____
  Dates taken, from _____/_____/_____   to _____/_____/_____
  Prescribing Physician _____
  Prescribing Physician Phone Number _____
  Prescribed for this Condition _____
  Pharmacy/Pharmacist Name _____
  Phone Number _____   Prescription Number _____

- Rx Name _____ Dosage _____
  How often taken? _____
  Dates taken, from _____/_____/_____   to _____/_____/_____
  Prescribing Physician _____
  Prescribing Physician Phone Number _____
  Prescribed for this Condition _____
  Pharmacy/Pharmacist Name _____
  Phone Number _____   Prescription Number _____

- Rx Name _____ Dosage _____
  How often taken? _____
  Dates taken, from _____/_____/_____   to _____/_____/_____
  Prescribing Physician _____
  Prescribing Physician Phone Number _____
  Prescribed for this Condition _____
  Pharmacy/Pharmacist Name _____
  Phone Number _____   Prescription Number _____

Detailed Non-Recurring Medication List

- Rx Name _____ Dosage _____
  How often taken? _____
  Dates taken, from _____/_____/_____ to _____/_____/_____
  Prescribing Physician _____
  Prescribing Physician Phone Number _____
  Prescribed for this Condition _____
  Pharmacy/Pharmacist Name _____
  Phone Number _____ Prescription Number _____

- Rx Name _____ Dosage _____
  How often taken? _____
  Dates taken, from _____/_____/_____ to _____/_____/_____
  Prescribing Physician _____
  Prescribing Physician Phone Number _____
  Prescribed for this Condition _____
  Pharmacy/Pharmacist Name _____
  Phone Number _____ Prescription Number _____

- Rx Name _____ Dosage _____
  How often taken? _____
  Dates taken, from _____/_____/_____ to _____/_____/_____
  Prescribing Physician _____
  Prescribing Physician Phone Number _____
  Prescribed for this Condition _____
  Pharmacy/Pharmacist Name _____
  Phone Number _____ Prescription Number _____

- Rx Name _____ Dosage _____
  How often taken? _____
  Dates taken, from _____/_____/_____ to _____/_____/_____
  Prescribing Physician _____
  Prescribing Physician Phone Number _____
  Prescribed for this Condition _____
  Pharmacy/Pharmacist Name _____
  Phone Number _____ Prescription Number _____

- Rx Name _____ Dosage _____
  How often taken? _____
  Dates taken, from _____/_____/_____ to _____/_____/_____
  Prescribing Physician _____
  Prescribing Physician Phone Number _____
  Prescribed for this Condition _____
  Pharmacy/Pharmacist Name _____
  Phone Number _____ Prescription Number _____

- Rx Name _____ Dosage _____
  How often taken? _____
  Dates taken, from _____/_____/_____ to _____/_____/_____
  Prescribing Physician _____
  Prescribing Physician Phone Number _____
  Prescribed for this Condition _____
  Pharmacy/Pharmacist Name _____
  Phone Number _____ Prescription Number _____

- Rx Name _____ Dosage _____
  How often taken? _____
  Dates taken, from _____/_____/_____ to _____/_____/_____
  Prescribing Physician _____
  Prescribing Physician Phone Number _____
  Prescribed for this Condition _____
  Pharmacy/Pharmacist Name _____
  Phone Number _____ Prescription Number _____

- Rx Name _____ Dosage _____
  How often taken? _____
  Dates taken, from _____/_____/_____ to _____/_____/_____
  Prescribing Physician _____
  Prescribing Physician Phone Number _____
  Prescribed for this Condition _____
  Pharmacy/Pharmacist Name _____
  Phone Number _____ Prescription Number _____

- Rx Name _____ Dosage _____
  How often taken? _____
  Dates taken, from _____/_____/_____ to _____/_____/_____
  Prescribing Physician _____
  Prescribing Physician Phone Number _____
  Prescribed for this Condition _____
  Pharmacy/Pharmacist Name _____
  Phone Number _____ Prescription Number _____

- Rx Name _____ Dosage _____
  How often taken? _____
  Dates taken, from _____/_____/_____ to _____/_____/_____
  Prescribing Physician _____
  Prescribing Physician Phone Number _____
  Prescribed for this Condition _____
  Pharmacy/Pharmacist Name _____
  Phone Number _____ Prescription Number _____

- Rx Name _____ Dosage _____
  How often taken? _____
  Dates taken, from _____/_____/_____ to _____/_____/_____
  Prescribing Physician _____
  Prescribing Physician Phone Number _____
  Prescribed for this Condition _____
  Pharmacy/Pharmacist Name _____
  Phone Number _____ Prescription Number _____

- Rx Name _____ Dosage _____
  How often taken? _____
  Dates taken, from _____/_____/_____ to _____/_____/_____
  Prescribing Physician _____
  Prescribing Physician Phone Number _____
  Prescribed for this Condition _____
  Pharmacy/Pharmacist Name _____
  Phone Number _____ Prescription Number _____

- Rx Name _____ Dosage _____
  How often taken? _____
  Dates taken, from _____/_____/_____ to _____/_____/_____
  Prescribing Physician _____
  Prescribing Physician Phone Number _____
  Prescribed for this Condition _____
  Pharmacy/Pharmacist Name _____
  Phone Number _____ Prescription Number _____

- Rx Name _____ Dosage _____
  How often taken? _____
  Dates taken, from _____/_____/_____ to _____/_____/_____
  Prescribing Physician _____
  Prescribing Physician Phone Number _____
  Prescribed for this Condition _____
  Pharmacy/Pharmacist Name _____
  Phone Number _____ Prescription Number _____

- Rx Name _____ Dosage _____
  How often taken? _____
  Dates taken, from _____/_____/_____ to _____/_____/_____
  Prescribing Physician _____
  Prescribing Physician Phone Number _____
  Prescribed for this Condition _____
  Pharmacy/Pharmacist Name _____
  Phone Number _____ Prescription Number _____

- Rx Name _____ Dosage _____
  How often taken? _____
  Dates taken, from _____/_____/_____ to _____/_____/_____
  Prescribing Physician _____
  Prescribing Physician Phone Number _____
  Prescribed for this Condition _____
  Pharmacy/Pharmacist Name _____
  Phone Number _____ Prescription Number _____

- Rx Name _____ Dosage _____
  How often taken? _____
  Dates taken, from _____/_____/_____ to _____/_____/_____
  Prescribing Physician _____
  Prescribing Physician Phone Number _____
  Prescribed for this Condition _____
  Pharmacy/Pharmacist Name _____
  Phone Number _____ Prescription Number _____

- Rx Name _____ Dosage _____
  How often taken? _____
  Dates taken, from _____/_____/_____ to _____/_____/_____
  Prescribing Physician _____
  Prescribing Physician Phone Number _____
  Prescribed for this Condition _____
  Pharmacy/Pharmacist Name _____
  Phone Number _____ Prescription Number _____

- Rx Name _____ Dosage _____
  How often taken? _____
  Dates taken, from _____/_____/_____ to _____/_____/_____
  Prescribing Physician _____
  Prescribing Physician Phone Number _____
  Prescribed for this Condition _____
  Pharmacy/Pharmacist Name _____
  Phone Number _____ Prescription Number _____

- Rx Name _____ Dosage _____
  How often taken? _____
  Dates taken, from _____/_____/_____ to _____/_____/_____
  Prescribing Physician _____
  Prescribing Physician Phone Number _____
  Prescribed for this Condition _____
  Pharmacy/Pharmacist Name _____
  Phone Number _____ Prescription Number _____

- Rx Name _____ Dosage _____
  How often taken? _____
  Dates taken, from _____/_____/_____ to _____/_____/_____
  Prescribing Physician _____
  Prescribing Physician Phone Number _____
  Prescribed for this Condition _____
  Pharmacy/Pharmacist Name _____
  Phone Number _____ Prescription Number _____

- Rx Name _____ Dosage _____
  How often taken? _____
  Dates taken, from _____/_____/_____ to _____/_____/_____
  Prescribing Physician _____
  Prescribing Physician Phone Number _____
  Prescribed for this Condition _____
  Pharmacy/Pharmacist Name _____
  Phone Number _____ Prescription Number _____

- Rx Name _____ Dosage _____
  How often taken? _____
  Dates taken, from _____/_____/_____ to _____/_____/_____
  Prescribing Physician _____
  Prescribing Physician Phone Number _____
  Prescribed for this Condition _____
  Pharmacy/Pharmacist Name _____
  Phone Number _____ Prescription Number _____

- Rx Name _____ Dosage _____
  How often taken? _____
  Dates taken, from _____/_____/_____ to _____/_____/_____
  Prescribing Physician _____
  Prescribing Physician Phone Number _____
  Prescribed for this Condition _____
  Pharmacy/Pharmacist Name _____
  Phone Number _____ Prescription Number _____

Current Care Providers

Home Care Company:

Name _____

Address/Location_____

Contact Name _____ Phone Number _____

Fax Number _____ Email _____

Cost $_____/month

Payment Source

    [ ]   Veterans Benefits   [ ]   Health Insurance

    [ ]   Long Term Care Insurance   [ ]   Private Pay

    [ ]   Medicaid/Medi-Cal/State or Government Program

    [ ]   Other _____

    [ ]   Other _____

Automatic Payments? _____ yes _____ no

Paid From Which Account? _____

Billing Manager/Contact Person _____

Billing Contact Phone Number _____

Home Health Company:

Name _____

Address/Location_____

Contact Name _____ Phone Number _____

Fax Number _____ Email _____

Cost $_____/month

Payment Source

    [ ]   Veterans Benefits   [ ]   Health Insurance

    [ ]   Long Term Care Insurance   [ ]   Private Pay

    [ ]   Medicaid/Medi-Cal/State or Government Program

    [ ]   Other _____

    [ ]   Other _____

Automatic Payments? _____ yes _____ no

Paid From Which Account? _____

Billing Manager/Contact Person _____

Billing Contact Phone Number _____

Hospice:

    Name _____

    Address/Location_____

    Contact Name _____ Phone Number _____

    Fax Number _____ Email _____

    Cost $_____/month

    Payment Source

        [ ]   Veterans Benefits   [ ]   Health Insurance

        [ ]   Long Term Care Insurance   [ ]   Private Pay

        [ ]   Medicaid/Medi-Cal/State or Government Program

        [ ]   Other _____

        [ ]   Other _____

    Automatic Payments? _____ yes _____ no

    Paid From Which Account? _____

    Billing Manager/Contact Person _____

    Billing Contact Phone Number _____

Home Health Company:

    Name _____

    Address/Location_____

    Contact Name _____ Phone Number _____

    Fax Number _____ Email _____

    Cost $_____/month

    Payment Source

        [ ]   Veterans Benefits   [ ]   Health Insurance

        [ ]   Long Term Care Insurance   [ ]   Private Pay

        [ ]   Medicaid/Medi-Cal/State or Government Program

        [ ]   Other _____

        [ ]   Other _____

    Automatic Payments? _____ yes _____ no

    Paid From Which Account? _____

    Billing Manager/Contact Person _____

    Billing Contact Phone Number _____

Adult Daycare Services:

Name _____

Address/Location_____

Contact Name _____ Phone Number _____

Fax Number _____ Email _____

Cost $_____/month

Payment Source

    [ ]   Veterans Benefits   [ ]   Health Insurance

    [ ]   Long Term Care Insurance   [ ]   Private Pay

    [ ]   Medicaid/Medi-Cal/State or Government Program

    [ ]   Other _____

    [ ]   Other _____

Automatic Payments? _____ yes _____ no

Paid From Which Account? _____

Billing Manager/Contact Person _____

Billing Contact Phone Number _____

Other Care Provider:

Name _____

Address/Location_____

Contact Name _____ Phone Number _____

Fax Number _____ Email _____

Cost $_____/month

Payment Source

    [ ]   Veterans Benefits   [ ]   Health Insurance

    [ ]   Long Term Care Insurance   [ ]   Private Pay

    [ ]   Medicaid/Medi-Cal/State or Government Program

    [ ]   Other _____

    [ ]   Other _____

Automatic Payments? _____ yes _____ no

Paid From Which Account? _____

Billing Manager/Contact Person _____

Billing Contact Phone Number _____

Notes:

Notes:

_____

_____

_____

_____

_____

_____

_____

_____

_____

_____

_____

_____

_____

_____

_____

_____

_____

_____

_____

_____

_____

_____

_____

_____

_____

_____

_____

_____

_____

_____

Chapter 6

CURRENT LIVING SITUATION

My Story:

"I had a call from my dad's memory care assisted living facility. They said he was unresponsive and could not be awakened. Fearing a stroke, our family collected at the ER. The doctors then proceeded with a battery of tests. Dad was just lying there. He had a catheter inserted, blood drawn, a chest x-ray, CT scan, and other tests that I can't remember. Finally after several hours, the doctor came by to give us the news and we expected the worst. The doctor said that all the tests were negative (whew!) but then I asked, "So, what is wrong with him?" The doctor replied, "Nothing!" My response was, "…but he is not awake!", to which the doctor replied, "I know… because he is sleeping." Still unconscious, we transported my dad back to the assisted living facility where he was put back in bed. He woke up the next morning, refreshed and ready for the day. He did not have a clue that he went on this trip! I think I now know how some people think they have been abducted. My dad was abducted, went to the hospital for what amounted to a complete physical, went home, and had no knowledge of any of it!"

Where does your loved one live? _____ residence that he/she owns

_____ rented apartment/home/condo/etc.

_____ with a family member

_____ independent living home

_____ assisted living home

_____ memory care facility

_____ board and care facility/residential care home

_____ skilled nursing home/rehab

_____ other _____

Residence that Your Loved One Owns

Address _____ PhoneNumber_____

_____ Fax Number _____

Email(s) _____

Current Rental Apartment/Home/Condo/Etc.

Landlord/Property Manager Name _____

Address _____ PhoneNumber_____

_____ Fax Number _____

Email _____

Rent Amount $_____/month   Due Date _____ of each month

Payment Source for Rent (Account, etc.) _____

Renter's Insurance Company Name _____

Renter's Insurance Policy Number _____

Living With Family Member

Name _____ Relationship_____

Address _____ PhoneNumber_____

_____ Fax Number _____

Email _____

Current Independent Living Home

Name _____

Address _____ Phone Number _____

_____ Fax Number _____

Email _____

Date Entered Facility _____ Date Left Facility (if applicable) _____

Administrator Name _____ Phone Number _____

Executive Director Name _____ Phone Number _____

Med Tech Name _____ Phone Number _____

Nurse _____ Type [ ] RN [ ] LVN Shift Hours _____ to _____

Nurse _____ Type [ ] RN [ ] LVN Shift Hours _____ to _____

Nurse _____ Type [ ] RN [ ] LVN Shift Hours _____ to _____

Current Services Provided
- [ ] Room and Board
- [ ] Medicine Management
- [ ] Bathing
- [ ] Grooming
- [ ] Dressing
- [ ] Transferring (getting in and out of bed, etc.)
- [ ] Toileting
- [ ] Eating
- [ ] Drinking
- [ ] Other _____
- [ ] Other _____
- [ ] Other _____
- [ ] Other _____
- [ ] Other _____

Cost $_____/month

Payment Source
- [ ] Veterans Benefits
- [ ] Medicaid/Medi-Cal/State or Government Program
- [ ] Long Term Care Insurance
- [ ] Private Pay
- [ ] Other _____
- [ ] Other _____

Automatic Payments? _____ yes _____ no

Paid From Which Account? _____

Billing Manager/Contact Person _____

Billing Contact Phone Number _____

Current Assisted Living Home

Name _____

Address _____ Phone Number _____

_____ Fax Number _____

Email _____

Date Entered Facility _____ Date Left Facility (if applicable) _____

Administrator Name _____ Phone Number _____

Executive Director Name _____ Phone Number _____

Med Tech Name _____ Phone Number _____

Nurse _____ Type [ ] RN [ ] LVN Shift Hours _____ to _____

Nurse _____ Type [ ] RN [ ] LVN Shift Hours _____ to _____

Nurse _____ Type [ ] RN [ ] LVN Shift Hours _____ to _____

Current Services Provided   [ ]   Room and Board

[ ]   Medicine Management

[ ]   Bathing

[ ]   Grooming

[ ]   Dressing

[ ]   Transferring (getting in and out of bed, etc.)

[ ]   Toileting

[ ]   Eating

[ ]   Drinking

[ ]   Other _____

[ ]   Other _____

[ ]   Other _____

[ ]   Other _____

[ ]   Other _____

Cost $_____/month

Payment Source   [ ]   Veterans Benefits

[ ]   Medicaid/Medi-Cal/State or Government Program

[ ]   Long Term Care Insurance

[ ]   Private Pay

[ ]   Other _____

[ ]   Other _____

Automatic Payments? _____ yes _____ no

Paid From Which Account? _____

Billing Manager/Contact Person _____

Billing Contact Phone Number _____

Current Memory Care Facility

Name _____

Address _____ Phone Number _____

_____ Fax Number _____

Email _____

Date Entered Facility _____ Date Left Facility (if applicable) _____

Administrator Name _____ Phone Number _____

Executive Director Name _____ Phone Number _____

Med Tech Name _____ Phone Number _____

Nurse _____ Type [ ] RN [ ] LVN Shift Hours _____ to _____

Nurse _____ Type [ ] RN [ ] LVN Shift Hours _____ to _____

Nurse _____ Type [ ] RN [ ] LVN Shift Hours _____ to _____

Current Services Provided   [ ]   Room and Board

                                    [ ]   Medicine Management

                                    [ ]   Bathing

                                    [ ]   Grooming

                                    [ ]   Dressing

                                    [ ]   Transferring (getting in and out of bed, etc.)

                                    [ ]   Toileting

                                    [ ]   Eating

                                    [ ]   Drinking

                                    [ ]   Other _____

                                    [ ]   Other _____

                                    [ ]   Other _____

                                    [ ]   Other _____

                                    [ ]   Other _____

Cost $_____/month

Payment Source   [ ]   Veterans Benefits

                                    [ ]   Medicaid/Medi-Cal/State or Government Program

                                    [ ]   Long Term Care Insurance

                                    [ ]   Private Pay

                                    [ ]   Other _____

                                    [ ]   Other _____

Automatic Payments? _____ yes _____ no

Paid From Which Account? _____

Billing Manager/Contact Person _____

Billing Contact Phone Number _____

Current Board & Care Facility or Residential Care Home

Name _____

Address _____ Phone Number _____

_____ Fax Number _____

Email _____

Date Entered Facility _____ Date Left Facility (if applicable) _____

Administrator Name _____ Phone Number _____

Executive Director Name _____ Phone Number _____

Med Tech Name _____ Phone Number _____

Nurse _____ Type [ ] RN [ ] LVN Shift Hours _____ to _____

Nurse _____ Type [ ] RN [ ] LVN Shift Hours _____ to _____

Nurse _____ Type [ ] RN [ ] LVN Shift Hours _____ to _____

Current Services Provided
- [ ] Room and Board
- [ ] Medicine Management
- [ ] Bathing
- [ ] Grooming
- [ ] Dressing
- [ ] Transferring (getting in and out of bed, etc.)
- [ ] Toileting
- [ ] Eating
- [ ] Drinking
- [ ] Other _____
- [ ] Other _____
- [ ] Other _____
- [ ] Other _____
- [ ] Other _____

Cost $_____/month

Payment Source
- [ ] Veterans Benefits
- [ ] Medicaid/Medi-Cal/State or Government Program
- [ ] Long Term Care Insurance
- [ ] Private Pay
- [ ] Other _____
- [ ] Other _____

Automatic Payments? _____ yes _____ no

Paid From Which Account? _____

Billing Manager/Contact Person _____

Billing Contact Phone Number _____

Current Skilled Nursing Home or Rehab Facility

Name _____

Address _____ Phone Number _____

_____ Fax Number _____

Email _____

Date Entered Facility _____ Date Left Facility (if applicable) _____

Admitting Physician Name _____ Phone Number _____

Administrator Name _____ Phone Number _____

Executive Director Name _____ Phone Number _____

Med Tech Name _____ Phone Number _____

Physician Name _____ Phone Number _____

Physician Name _____ Phone Number _____

Nurse _____ Type [ ] RN [ ] LVN Shift Hours _____ to _____

Nurse _____ Type [ ] RN [ ] LVN Shift Hours _____ to _____

Nurse _____ Type [ ] RN [ ] LVN Shift Hours _____ to _____

Cost $_____/month

Payment Source

[ ]   Veterans Benefits
[ ]   Medicaid/Medi-Cal/State or Government Program
[ ]   Long Term Care Insurance
[ ]   Private Pay
[ ]   Health Insurance Policy
[ ]   Medicare
[ ]   Private Pay
[ ]   Other _____
[ ]   Other _____

Automatic Payments? _____ yes _____ no

Paid From Which Account? _____

Billing Manager/Contact Person _____

Billing Contact Phone Number _____

Notes _____

_____
_____
_____
_____
_____
_____
_____

Other Residence or Facility

Name _____

Address _____ Phone Number _____

_____ Fax Number _____

Email _____

Date Entered Facility _____ Date Left Facility (if applicable) _____

Administrator Name _____ Phone Number _____

Executive Director Name _____ Phone Number _____

Med Tech Name _____ Phone Number _____

Nurse _____ Type [ ] RN [ ] LVN Shift Hours _____ to _____

Nurse _____ Type [ ] RN [ ] LVN Shift Hours _____ to _____

Nurse _____ Type [ ] RN [ ] LVN Shift Hours _____ to _____

Current Services Provided

[ ]   Room and Board

[ ]   Medicine Management

[ ]   Bathing

[ ]   Grooming

[ ]   Dressing

[ ]   Transferring (getting in and out of bed, etc.)

[ ]   Toileting

[ ]   Eating

[ ]   Drinking

[ ]   Other _____

[ ]   Other _____

[ ]   Other _____

[ ]   Other _____

[ ]   Other _____

Cost $_____/month

Payment Source

[ ]   Veterans Benefits

[ ]   Medicaid/Medi-Cal/State or Government Program

[ ]   Long Term Care Insurance

[ ]   Private Pay

[ ]   Other _____

[ ]   Other _____

Automatic Payments? _____ yes _____ no

Paid From Which Account? _____

Billing Manager/Contact Person _____

Billing Contact Phone Number _____

Notes:

_____
_____
_____
_____
_____
_____
_____
_____
_____
_____
_____
_____
_____
_____
_____
_____
_____
_____
_____
_____
_____
_____
_____
_____
_____
_____
_____
_____
_____
_____
_____
_____
_____

Notes:

Chapter 7

DESIRED OR PRE-SELECTED FACILITIES & SERVICE PROVIDERS

My Story:

"I live in San Diego County, California, which can turn into a tinderbox if there is less than the normal amount of rain during the year. Recently we had eight wildfires flaming at the same time. Getting a call for you to evacuate your own home is one thing, but getting another call to evacuate your mother in assisted living is another thing. How about if there is more than one parent in assisted living? Medicines, diapers, food, clothes, walkers, and your parent's own panic to deal with as well! Plan ahead for events like this if you are in an area prone to natural disasters."

Desired or Pre-Selected Facilities & Service Providers

I remember when my mother-in-law broke her hip and was being discharged from the hospital to a rehabilitation center (basically a nursing home for therapy). The discharge planner at the hospital gave us a list of local facilities and asked us to pick one. Of course, we asked which facility was the best one for her to go to and her response was that she couldn't tell us or give us any information, as it would be against the law and/or hospital policy. Unfortunately our first choice was a disaster and it took several horrible days before we could get her transferred to another facility.

This experience alerted me to a problem, and thus this section is designed to determine the elder's desired facilities or service providers. You generally do not have the luxury of time to research, visit and select a location or service when these decisions need to be made (usually during an emergency). The best plan is to select these providers well in advance and have them ready to go if and when the need arises. It is often surprising to see how often the elder will need to go to one or more of these facilities or providers, so be prepared.

In Case of Emergency, Desired Evacuation Place:

Name _____

Address/Location_____

Contact Person _____ Phone Number _____

Contact Cell Number _____ Contact Fax Number _____

Contact Email _____

Hospital:

Name _____

Address/Location_____

Phone Number _____ Fax Number _____

ER Phone Number _____

Rehabilitation Facility:

    Name _____

    Address/Location_____

    Administrator Name _____ Phone Number _____

    Fax Number _____ Email _____

    Accepts Medicaid/Medi-Cal? [   ] yes   [   ] no

Skilled Nursing Facility:

    Name _____

    Address/Location_____

    Administrator Name _____ Phone Number _____

    Fax Number _____ Email _____

    Accepts Medicaid/Medi-Cal? [   ] yes   [   ] no

Memory Care Facility:

    Name _____

    Address/Location_____

    Administrator Name _____ Phone Number _____

    Fax Number _____ Email _____

    Accepts Medicaid/Medi-Cal? [   ] yes   [   ] no

Assisted Living Facility:

    Name _____

    Address/Location_____

    Administrator Name _____ Phone Number _____

    Fax Number _____ Email _____

    Accepts Medicaid/Medi-Cal? [   ] yes   [   ] no

Independent Living Facility:

    Name _____

    Address/Location_____

    Administrator Name _____ Phone Number _____

    Fax Number _____ Email _____

    Accepts Medicaid/Medi-Cal? [   ] yes   [   ] no

Board and Care/Residential Care Facility:

    Name _____

    Address/Location_____

    Administrator Name _____ Phone Number _____

    Fax Number _____ Email _____

    Accepts Medicaid/Medi-Cal? [   ] yes   [   ] no

Hospice:

Name _____

Address/Location_____

Contact Name _____ Phone Number _____

Fax Number _____ Email _____

Accepts Medicaid/Medi-Cal? [ ] yes [ ] no

Home Care Company:

Name _____

Address/Location_____

Contact Name _____ Phone Number _____

Fax Number _____ Email _____

Accepts Medicaid/Medi-Cal? [ ] yes [ ] no

Other:

Name _____

Address/Location_____

Contact Name _____ Phone Number _____

Fax Number _____ Email _____

Accepts Medicaid/Medi-Cal? [ ] yes [ ] no

Other:

Name _____

Address/Location_____

Contact Name _____ Phone Number _____

Fax Number _____ Email _____

Accepts Medicaid/Medi-Cal? [ ] yes [ ] no

Other:

Name _____

Address/Location_____

Contact Name _____ Phone Number _____

Fax Number _____ Email _____

Accepts Medicaid/Medi-Cal? [ ] yes [ ] no

Other:

Name _____

Address/Location_____

Contact Name _____ Phone Number _____

Fax Number _____ Email _____

Accepts Medicaid/Medi-Cal? [ ] yes [ ] no

Notes:

Notes:

Chapter 8

PETS

A Friend's Story:

"After the kids move out and grow up, seniors often become even more attached to their pets, and vice versa. My grandmother moved in to our house for a time, while she and my grandfather were looking for an assisted living community to move into. My small dog, who was always quite attached to me, gradually set aside our long friendship and decided to become best friends with my grandmother instead. You see, they both had a lot in common. Their favorite things to do were to take naps, relax, and eat. You can see why my grandmother and my dog got along so well. After my grandparents moved out, the dog moped for weeks. His best friend, and nap buddy, was gone. He wandered listlessly around the house for days. My grandmother missed living with him too (I think even more than she missed living with us!)."

Pets

Pets are the forgotten loved ones. In the event of an emergency, where will the pets be housed and cared for? Additionally if the elder has to move to quarters that do not allow his or her pet, or perhaps passes away, what arrangements have been made to adopt the elder's pet(s)?

This section is to give detailed instructions to the pet caretaker(s), whether in an emergency or on a permanent basis.

You may consider posting this information in the elder's room or residence to let first responders know whom to call if they need to separate the elder from their pet.

* * * *

1)   Pet Name   _____

        Type   dog   cat   other _____

        Breed   _____ Age _____ as of _____/_____/_____

        Weight   _____ Color _____

        Vet Name   _____ Phone Number _____

        Address   _____

        Vet Hospital   _____ Phone Number _____

        Address   _____

        Illnesses   _____ _____

        Rx Name   _____ For Treatment Of _____

                        dosage _____ How Often Taken? _____

        Rx Name   _____ For Treatment Of _____

                        dosage _____ How Often Taken? _____

        Rx Name   _____ For Treatment Of _____

                        dosage _____ How Often Taken? _____

        Tendencies? [ ] Aggressive to People   [ ] Aggressive to Animals

                     [ ] Potty Trained   [ ] Crate Trained

                     [ ] _____   [ ] _____

        Food Brand/Type _____ Quantity _____

        Feeding Intervals/Time (x per day) _____

        Food Brand/Type _____ Quantity _____

        Feeding Intervals/Time (x per day) _____

        Regular/Permanent Location or Home _____

        _____

        Pet Sitter Name/Phone Number _____

        _____

        Microchip/Tracker ID Number/Phone Number _____

        _____

        Emergency Contact Person/Phone Number & Desired Location _____

        _____

        Notes: _____

        _____

        _____

        _____

        _____

        _____

        _____

2)   Pet Name   _____

Type   dog   cat   other _____

Breed   _____ Age _____ as of _____/_____/_____

Weight   _____ Color _____

Vet Name   _____ Phone Number _____

Address   _____

Vet Hospital   _____ Phone Number _____

Address   _____

Illnesses   _____ _____

Rx Name   _____ For Treatment Of _____

                dosage _____ How Often Taken? _____

Rx Name   _____ For Treatment Of _____

                dosage _____ How Often Taken? _____

Rx Name   _____ For Treatment Of _____

                dosage _____ How Often Taken? _____

Tendencies? [ ] Aggressive to People   [ ] Aggressive to Animals
             [ ] Potty Trained   [ ] Crate Trained
             [ ] _____   [ ] _____

Food Brand/Type _____ Quantity _____

Feeding Intervals/Time (x per day) _____

Food Brand/Type _____ Quantity _____

Feeding Intervals/Time (x per day) _____

Regular/Permanent Location or Home _____

_____

Pet Sitter Name/Phone Number _____

_____

Microchip/Tracker ID Number/Phone Number _____

_____

Emergency Contact Person/Phone Number & Desired Location _____

_____

Notes: _____

_____

_____

_____

_____

_____

_____

3) Pet Name   _____

Type   dog   cat   other _____

Breed   _____ Age _____ as of _____/_____/_____

Weight   _____ Color _____

Vet Name   _____ Phone Number _____

Address   _____

Vet Hospital _____ Phone Number _____

Address   _____

Illnesses   _____ _____

Rx Name   _____ For Treatment Of _____

             dosage _____ How Often Taken? _____

Rx Name   _____ For Treatment Of _____

             dosage _____ How Often Taken? _____

Rx Name   _____ For Treatment Of _____

             dosage _____ How Often Taken? _____

Tendencies? [ ] Aggressive to People   [ ] Aggressive to Animals

             [ ] Potty Trained   [ ] Crate Trained

             [ ] _____   [ ] _____

Food Brand/Type _____ Quantity _____

Feeding Intervals/Time (x per day) _____

Food Brand/Type _____ Quantity _____

Feeding Intervals/Time (x per day) _____

Regular/Permanent Location or Home _____

_____

Pet Sitter Name/Phone Number _____

_____

Microchip/Tracker ID Number/Phone Number _____

_____

Emergency Contact Person/Phone Number & Desired Location _____

_____

Notes: _____

_____

_____

_____

_____

_____

_____

4)   Pet Name   _____

Type   dog   cat   other _____

Breed   _____   Age _____ as of _____/_____/_____

Weight   _____   Color _____

Vet Name   _____   Phone Number _____

Address   _____

Vet Hospital _____   Phone Number _____

Address   _____

Illnesses   _____   _____

Rx Name   _____   For Treatment Of _____

              dosage _____   How Often Taken? _____

Rx Name   _____   For Treatment Of _____

              dosage _____   How Often Taken? _____

Rx Name   _____   For Treatment Of _____

              dosage _____   How Often Taken? _____

Tendencies? [ ] Aggressive to People   [ ] Aggressive to Animals

             [ ] Potty Trained   [ ] Crate Trained

             [ ] _____   [ ] _____

Food Brand/Type _____   Quantity _____

Feeding Intervals/Time (x per day) _____

Food Brand/Type _____   Quantity _____

Feeding Intervals/Time (x per day) _____

Regular/Permanent Location or Home _____

_____

Pet Sitter Name/Phone Number _____

_____

Microchip/Tracker ID Number/Phone Number _____

_____

Emergency Contact Person/Phone Number & Desired Location _____

_____

Notes: _____

_____

_____

_____

_____

_____

_____

5)   Pet Name   _____

        Type   dog   cat   other _____

        Breed   _____ Age _____ as of _____/_____/_____

        Weight   _____ Color _____

        Vet Name   _____ Phone Number _____

        Address   _____

        Vet Hospital _____ Phone Number _____

        Address   _____

        Illnesses   _____ _____

        Rx Name   _____ For Treatment Of _____

                      dosage _____ How Often Taken? _____

        Rx Name   _____ For Treatment Of _____

                      dosage _____ How Often Taken? _____

        Rx Name   _____ For Treatment Of _____

                      dosage _____ How Often Taken? _____

        Tendencies? [ ] Aggressive to People   [ ] Aggressive to Animals

                     [ ] Potty Trained   [ ] Crate Trained

                     [ ] _____   [ ] _____

        Food Brand/Type _____ Quantity _____

        Feeding Intervals/Time (x per day) _____

        Food Brand/Type _____ Quantity _____

        Feeding Intervals/Time (x per day) _____

        Regular/Permanent Location or Home _____

        _____

        Pet Sitter Name/Phone Number _____

        _____

        Microchip/Tracker ID Number/Phone Number _____

        _____

        Emergency Contact Person/Phone Number & Desired Location _____

        _____

        Notes: _____

        _____

        _____

        _____

        _____

        _____

        _____

6) Pet Name _____

Type   dog   cat   other _____

Breed _____ Age _____ as of _____/_____/_____

Weight _____ Color _____

Vet Name _____ Phone Number _____

Address _____

Vet Hospital _____ Phone Number _____

Address _____

Illnesses _____ _____

Rx Name _____ For Treatment Of _____

dosage _____ How Often Taken? _____

Rx Name _____ For Treatment Of _____

dosage _____ How Often Taken? _____

Rx Name _____ For Treatment Of _____

dosage _____ How Often Taken? _____

Tendencies? [ ] Aggressive to People   [ ] Aggressive to Animals

              [ ] Potty Trained   [ ] Crate Trained

              [ ] _____   [ ] _____

Food Brand/Type _____ Quantity _____

Feeding Intervals/Time (x per day) _____

Food Brand/Type _____ Quantity _____

Feeding Intervals/Time (x per day) _____

Regular/Permanent Location or Home _____

_____

Pet Sitter Name/Phone Number _____

_____

Microchip/Tracker ID Number/Phone Number _____

_____

Emergency Contact Person/Phone Number & Desired Location _____

_____

Notes: _____

_____

_____

_____

_____

_____

_____

Notes:

_____

_____

_____

_____

_____

_____

_____

_____

_____

_____

_____

_____

_____

_____

_____

_____

_____

_____

_____

_____

_____

_____

_____

_____

_____

_____

_____

_____

_____

Notes:

Chapter 9

FINANCIAL INFORMATION

A Friend's Story:

"Many seniors need help managing their finances. A good friend of mine was caring for her great aunt for a number of years and as time went by, she gradually took over her financial work for her, paying bills, etc. since the aunt was unable to keep track of everything with her failing memory. Despite the legal and financial documents that the aunt had put in place years earlier, allowing her niece to do her banking for her, there was one time when the bank insisted that the great aunt come in personally to authorize a specific transaction. By this time, the aunt had reached the grand age of 96, and her long term memory was long gone due to Alzheimer's Disease. The banker ended up regretting insisting that the aunt visit the bank herself, since the 96 year old woman instantly berated him for making her, "The Queen of Sheba," visit the bank personally. Apparently, during memory lapses the great aunt sometimes decided that she was a biblical monarch, and there wasn't anything that would sway her mind when she got started. You never know what situations you are going to run into when you are helping an elder, even with something as mundane as a visit to the bank."

Financial Information

This section may be the most monotonous to complete but it gives the reader a great snapshot of the financial situation of the elder.

Remember that it may not be you that is trying to identify assets and manage them in a particular situation. You may be out of town, sick, or just otherwise unable to handle a particular issue. This book can easily be given to a sibling, or trusted friend or advisor and they have all the financial information readily at hand.

Particularly for this section, it is important to remember that great care must be taken to keep this book from theft or viewing by unauthorized persons. This book is a great tool to be able to help manage an elder's needs, but the vital information that it contains is sensitive in nature and potentially dangerous in the wrong hands. Keep it safe!

Financial information changes often, so remember to keep this section (and other sections of the *ElderCare Ready Pack*) updated often so that you have the most relevant and helpful information at hand.

* * * *

Real Property

Residence

Address _____

County _____

Value $ _____ (estimated current fair market value)

               $ _____ (current assessed total value from county assessor)

Loans $ _____ (current total of all loans on property)

Property Tax $ _____/annually for year 20_____

Assessor's Parcel Number(APN)/Parcel Identifier Number _____

Name of Owner on Title _____

Homeowners Insurance Policy Company _____

    Homeowners Insurance Policy Number _____

    Homeowners Insurance Payment Method [ ] Impound Account [ ] Paid By Borrower

Homeowners Association (HOA) Name _____

    HOA Association Phone Number _____

    HOA Fees Amount $ _____ paid each _____ (year, month, etc.)

Type of Property

    [ ] Single Family Residence   [ ] Trailer w/o Land   [ ] Trailer w/Land

    [ ] Mobile Home w/o Land   [ ] Mobile Home w/Land [ ] Condo/Apartment

    [ ] Timeshare   [ ] Other _____

Mortgage Lender/Company Name _____

    Lender Phone Number _____

    Name of Borrower on Loan _____

    Statement Address _____

    Loan Number _____ Payment Amount _____/month

    Amount Owed as of date _____/_____/_____ is $ _____

    [ ] Release on File

Mortgage Lender/Company Name _____

    Lender Phone Number _____

    Name of Borrower on Loan _____

    Statement Address _____

    Loan Number _____ Payment Amount _____/month

    Amount Owed as of date _____/_____/_____ is $ _____

    [ ] Release on File

Is this home rented? [ ] yes [ ] no   Rental Income Amount $ _____/month

    Tenant Name _____

    Tenant Phone Number _____ Tenant Email _____

<u>Other Real Estate</u>

Address _____

        County _____

Value $ _____ (estimated current fair market value)

           $ _____ (current assessed total value from county assessor)

Loans $ _____ (current total of all loans on property)

Property Tax $ _____/annually for year 20_____

Assessor's Parcel Number(APN)/Parcel Identifier Number _____

Name of Owner on Title _____

Homeowners Insurance Policy Company _____

     Homeowners Insurance Policy Number _____

     Homeowners Insurance Payment Method [ ] Impound Account [ ] Paid By Borrower

Homeowners Association (HOA) Name _____

     HOA Association Phone Number _____

     HOA Fees Amount $ _____ paid each _____ (year, month, etc.)

Type of Property

     [ ] Single Family Residence   [ ] Trailer w/o Land   [ ] Trailer w/Land

     [ ] Mobile Home w/o Land   [ ] Mobile Home w/Land [ ] Condo/Apartment

     [ ] Timeshare   [ ] Other _____

Mortgage Lender/Company Name _____

     Lender Phone Number _____

     Name of Borrower on Loan _____

     Statement Address _____

     Loan Number _____ Payment Amount _____/month

     Amount Owed as of date _____/_____/_____ is $ _____

     [ ] Release on File

Mortgage Lender/Company Name _____

     Lender Phone Number _____

     Name of Borrower on Loan _____

     Statement Address _____

     Loan Number _____ Payment Amount _____/month

     Amount Owed as of date _____/_____/_____ is $ _____

     [ ] Release on File

Is this home rented? [ ] yes [ ] no Rental Income Amount $ _____/month

     Tenant Name _____

     Tenant Phone Number _____ Tenant Email _____

Other Real Estate

Address   _____

        County _____

Value $ _____ (estimated current fair market value)

        $ _____ (current assessed total value from county assessor)

Loans $ _____ (current total of all loans on property)

Property Tax $ _____/annually for year 20_____

Assessor's Parcel Number(APN)/Parcel Identifier Number _____

Name of Owner on Title _____

Homeowners Insurance Policy Company _____

    Homeowners Insurance Policy Number _____

    Homeowners Insurance Payment Method [ ] Impound Account [ ] Paid By Borrower

Homeowners Association (HOA) Name _____

    HOA Association Phone Number _____

    HOA Fees Amount $ _____ paid each _____ (year, month, etc.)

Type of Property

    [ ] Single Family Residence   [ ] Trailer w/o Land   [ ] Trailer w/Land

    [ ] Mobile Home w/o Land   [ ] Mobile Home w/Land [ ] Condo/Apartment

    [ ] Timeshare   [ ] Other _____

Mortgage Lender/Company Name _____

    Lender Phone Number _____

    Name of Borrower on Loan _____

    Statement Address _____

    Loan Number _____ Payment Amount _____/month

    Amount Owed as of date _____/_____/_____ is $ _____

    [ ] Release on File

Mortgage Lender/Company Name _____

    Lender Phone Number _____

    Name of Borrower on Loan _____

    Statement Address _____

    Loan Number _____ Payment Amount _____/month

    Amount Owed as of date _____/_____/_____ is $ _____

    [ ] Release on File

Is this home rented? [ ] yes [ ] no   Rental Income Amount $ _____/month

    Tenant Name _____

    Tenant Phone Number _____ Tenant Email _____

<u>Other Real Estate</u>

Address _____

        County _____

Value $ _____ (estimated current fair market value)

        $ _____ (current assessed total value from county assessor)

Loans $ _____ (current total of all loans on property)

Property Tax $ _____/annually for year 20_____

Assessor's Parcel Number(APN)/Parcel Identifier Number _____

Name of Owner on Title _____

Homeowners Insurance Policy Company _____

    Homeowners Insurance Policy Number _____

    Homeowners Insurance Payment Method [ ] Impound Account [ ] Paid By Borrower

Homeowners Association (HOA) Name _____

    HOA Association Phone Number _____

    HOA Fees Amount $ _____ paid each _____ (year, month, etc.)

Type of Property

    [ ] Single Family Residence   [ ] Trailer w/o Land   [ ] Trailer w/Land

    [ ] Mobile Home w/o Land   [ ] Mobile Home w/Land [ ] Condo/Apartment

    [ ] Timeshare   [ ] Other _____

Mortgage Lender/Company Name _____

    Lender Phone Number _____

    Name of Borrower on Loan _____

    Statement Address _____

    Loan Number _____ Payment Amount _____/month

    Amount Owed as of date _____/_____/_____ is $ _____

    [ ] Release on File

Mortgage Lender/Company Name _____

    Lender Phone Number _____

    Name of Borrower on Loan _____

    Statement Address _____

    Loan Number _____ Payment Amount _____/month

    Amount Owed as of date _____/_____/_____ is $ _____

    [ ] Release on File

Is this home rented? [ ] yes [ ] no   Rental Income Amount $ _____/month

    Tenant Name _____

    Tenant Phone Number _____ Tenant Email _____

Bank Accounts

Bank Name _____

      Account Nickname _____

      Account Number _____

      Branch Address _____

      Branch Phone Number _____

      Customer Service Phone Number _____

Type of Account   [ ] Checking   [ ] Savings

                   [ ] Money Market   [ ] IRA/401(k)

                   [ ] CD/Time Deposit

                   [ ] Non-Retirement Account

                   [ ] Other Retirement Account

                   [ ] Fiduciary Account

                   [ ] Other _____

Owner Name(s) on Account _____

_____

Average Balance in Account $_____

Automatic Deposits

               [ ] Social Security   Amount $_____/month

               [ ] Social Security   Amount $_____/month

               [ ] Pension _____   Amount $_____/month

               [ ] Pension _____   Amount $_____/month

               [ ] Retirement _____   Amount $_____/month

               [ ] Retirement _____   Amount $_____/month

               [ ] Other _____   Amount $_____/month

               [ ] Other _____   Amount $_____/month

Authorized Signer(s) on Account _____

_____

Statement Mailing Address   _____

_____

Debit Card Number   _____

      Debit Card PIN _____ Debit Card Expiration Date _____/_____/_____

      CCV Code/Code on Back of Card _____

Online Banking Username _____

Online Banking Password _____

Online Banking PIN (if applicable) _____

[ ] Release on File

Bank Name _____

    Account Nickname _____

    Account Number _____

    Branch Address _____

    Branch Phone Number _____

    Customer Service Phone Number _____

Type of Account   [ ] Checking   [ ] Savings

                  [ ] Money Market   [ ] IRA/401(k)

                  [ ] CD/Time Deposit

                  [ ] Non-Retirement Account

                  [ ] Other Retirement Account

                  [ ] Fiduciary Account

                  [ ] Other _____

Owner Name(s) on Account _____

_____

Average Balance in Account $_____

Automatic Deposits

    [ ] Social Security   Amount $_____/month

    [ ] Social Security   Amount $_____/month

    [ ] Pension _____ Amount $_____/month

    [ ] Pension _____ Amount $_____/month

    [ ] Retirement _____ Amount $_____/month

    [ ] Retirement _____ Amount $_____/month

    [ ] Other _____ Amount $_____/month

    [ ] Other _____ Amount $_____/month

Authorized Signer(s) on Account _____

_____

Statement Mailing Address   _____

_____

Debit Card Number   _____

    Debit Card PIN _____ Debit Card Expiration Date _____/_____/_____

    CCV Code/Code on Back of Card _____

Online Banking Username _____

Online Banking Password _____

Online Banking PIN (if applicable) _____

[ ] Release on File

Bank Name _____

    Account Nickname _____

    Account Number _____

    Branch Address _____

    Branch Phone Number _____

    Customer Service Phone Number _____

Type of Account   [ ] Checking   [ ] Savings

                  [ ] Money Market   [ ] IRA/401(k)

                  [ ] CD/Time Deposit

                  [ ] Non-Retirement Account

                  [ ] Other Retirement Account

                  [ ] Fiduciary Account

                  [ ] Other _____

Owner Name(s) on Account _____

_____

Average Balance in Account $_____

Automatic Deposits

        [ ] Social Security   Amount $_____/month

        [ ] Social Security   Amount $_____/month

        [ ] Pension _____   Amount $_____/month

        [ ] Pension _____   Amount $_____/month

        [ ] Retirement _____   Amount $_____/month

        [ ] Retirement _____   Amount $_____/month

        [ ] Other _____   Amount $_____/month

        [ ] Other _____   Amount $_____/month

Authorized Signer(s) on Account _____

_____

Statement Mailing Address _____

_____

Debit Card Number _____

    Debit Card PIN _____ Debit Card Expiration Date _____/_____/_____

    CCV Code/Code on Back of Card _____

Online Banking Username _____

Online Banking Password _____

Online Banking PIN (if applicable) _____

[ ] Release on File

Bank Name _____

    Account Nickname _____

    Account Number _____

    Branch Address _____

    Branch Phone Number _____

    Customer Service Phone Number _____

Type of Account   [ ] Checking   [ ] Savings

                    [ ] Money Market   [ ] IRA/401(k)

                    [ ] CD/Time Deposit

                    [ ] Non-Retirement Account

                    [ ] Other Retirement Account

                    [ ] Fiduciary Account

                    [ ] Other _____

Owner Name(s) on Account _____

                                    _____

Average Balance in Account $_____

Automatic Deposits

             [ ] Social Security   Amount $_____/month

             [ ] Social Security   Amount $_____/month

             [ ] Pension _____   Amount $_____/month

             [ ] Pension _____   Amount $_____/month

             [ ] Retirement _____ Amount $_____/month

             [ ] Retirement _____ Amount $_____/month

             [ ] Other _____   Amount $_____/month

             [ ] Other _____   Amount $_____/month

Authorized Signer(s) on Account _____

                                    _____

Statement Mailing Address   _____

                                    _____

Debit Card Number   _____

    Debit Card PIN _____ Debit Card Expiration Date _____/_____/_____

    CCV Code/Code on Back of Card _____

Online Banking Username _____

Online Banking Password _____

Online Banking PIN (if applicable) _____

[ ] Release on File

Brokerage Accounts

Brokerage Firm Name _____

    Advisor Name _____

    Account Nickname _____

    Account Number _____

    Branch Address _____

    Branch Phone Number _____

    Customer Service Phone Number _____

Type of Account   [ ] Money Market   [ ] IRA/401(k)

                [ ] Non-Retirement Account

                [ ] Other Retirement Account (Mutual Funds, etc.)

                [ ] Fiduciary Account

                [ ] Other _____

Owner Name(s) on Account _____

_____

Average Balance in Account $_____

Automatic Deposits

    [ ] Social Security   Amount $_____/month

    [ ] Social Security   Amount $_____/month

    [ ] Pension _____   Amount $_____/month

    [ ] Pension _____   Amount $_____/month

    [ ] Retirement _____   Amount $_____/month

    [ ] Retirement _____   Amount $_____/month

    [ ] Other _____   Amount $_____/month

    [ ] Other _____   Amount $_____/month

Authorized Signer(s) on Account _____

_____

Statement Mailing Address   _____

_____

Access Card Number   _____

    Access Card PIN _____ Debit Card Expiration Date _____/_____/_____

    CCV Code/Code on Back of Card _____

Online Banking Username _____

Online Banking Password _____

Online Banking PIN (if applicable) _____

[ ] Release on File

Brokerage Firm Name _____

    Advisor Name _____

    Account Nickname _____

    Account Number _____

    Branch Address _____

    Branch Phone Number _____

    Customer Service Phone Number _____

Type of Account   [ ] Money Market   [ ] IRA/401(k)

        [ ] Non-Retirement Account

        [ ] Other Retirement Account (Mutual Funds, etc.)

        [ ] Fiduciary Account

        [ ] Other _____

Owner Name(s) on Account _____

_____

Average Balance in Account $_____

Automatic Deposits

    [ ] Social Security   Amount $_____/month

    [ ] Social Security   Amount $_____/month

    [ ] Pension _____   Amount $_____/month

    [ ] Pension _____   Amount $_____/month

    [ ] Retirement _____   Amount $_____/month

    [ ] Retirement _____   Amount $_____/month

    [ ] Other _____   Amount $_____/month

    [ ] Other _____   Amount $_____/month

Authorized Signer(s) on Account _____

_____

Statement Mailing Address   _____

_____

Access Card Number   _____

    Access Card PIN _____ Debit Card Expiration Date _____/_____/_____

    CCV Code/Code on Back of Card _____

Online Banking Username _____

Online Banking Password _____

Online Banking PIN (if applicable) _____

[ ] Release on File

Brokerage Firm Name _____

    Advisor Name _____

    Account Nickname _____

    Account Number _____

    Branch Address _____

    Branch Phone Number _____

    Customer Service Phone Number _____

Type of Account   [ ] Money Market   [ ] IRA/401(k)

                 [ ] Non-Retirement Account

                 [ ] Other Retirement Account (Mutual Funds, etc.)

                 [ ] Fiduciary Account

                 [ ] Other _____

Owner Name(s) on Account _____

                                        _____

Average Balance in Account $_____

Automatic Deposits

            [ ] Social Security   Amount $_____/month

            [ ] Social Security   Amount $_____/month

            [ ] Pension _____   Amount $_____/month

            [ ] Pension _____   Amount $_____/month

            [ ] Retirement _____   Amount $_____/month

            [ ] Retirement _____   Amount $_____/month

            [ ] Other _____   Amount $_____/month

            [ ] Other _____   Amount $_____/month

Authorized Signer(s) on Account _____

                                        _____

Statement Mailing Address   _____

                                        _____

Access Card Number   _____

    Access Card PIN _____ Debit Card Expiration Date _____/_____/_____

    CCV Code/Code on Back of Card _____

Online Banking Username _____

Online Banking Password _____

Online Banking PIN (if applicable) _____

[ ] Release on File

Brokerage Firm Name _____

    Advisor Name _____

    Account Nickname _____

    Account Number _____

    Branch Address _____

    Branch Phone Number _____

    Customer Service Phone Number _____

Type of Account   [ ] Money Market   [ ] IRA/401(k)

                  [ ] Non-Retirement Account

                  [ ] Other Retirement Account (Mutual Funds, etc.)

                  [ ] Fiduciary Account

                  [ ] Other _____

Owner Name(s) on Account _____

_____

Average Balance in Account $_____

Automatic Deposits

    [ ] Social Security   Amount $_____/month

    [ ] Social Security   Amount $_____/month

    [ ] Pension _____   Amount $_____/month

    [ ] Pension _____   Amount $_____/month

    [ ] Retirement _____   Amount $_____/month

    [ ] Retirement _____   Amount $_____/month

    [ ] Other _____   Amount $_____/month

    [ ] Other _____   Amount $_____/month

Authorized Signer(s) on Account _____

_____

Statement Mailing Address _____

_____

Access Card Number _____

    Access Card PIN _____ Debit Card Expiration Date _____/_____/_____

    CCV Code/Code on Back of Card _____

Online Banking Username _____

Online Banking Password _____

Online Banking PIN (if applicable) _____

[ ] Release on File

Annuities

Company Name _____

    Account/Contract Number _____

    Location of Original Annuity Contract _____

    Company Address_____

    Company Phone Number _____

Type of Account   [ ] Deferred   [ ] Immediate

                [ ] IRA/401(k)/Retirement (Qualified)

                [ ] Non-Retirement (Non-Qualified)

                [ ] Other _____

Owner Name(s) on Account _____

Name of Annuitant(s) _____

Value of Annuity $_____, as of date _____/_____/_____

Authorized Signers on Account   _____

Statement Mailing Address   _____

                          _____

Online Banking Username   _____

Online Banking Password   _____

[ ] Release on File

Company Name _____

    Account/Contract Number _____

    Location of Original Annuity Contract _____

    Company Address_____

    Company Phone Number _____

Type of Account   [ ] Deferred   [ ] Immediate

                [ ] IRA/401(k)/Retirement (Qualified)

                [ ] Non-Retirement (Non-Qualified)

                [ ] Other _____

Owner Name(s) on Account _____

Name of Annuitant(s) _____

Value of Annuity $_____, as of date _____/_____/_____

Authorized Signers on Account   _____

Statement Mailing Address   _____

                          _____

Online Banking Username   _____

Online Banking Password   _____

[ ] Release on File

Company Name _____

    Account/Contract Number _____

    Location of Original Annuity Contract _____

    Company Address _____

    Company Phone Number _____

Type of Account   [ ] Deferred   [ ] Immediate

                [ ] IRA/401(k)/Retirement (Qualified)

                [ ] Non-Retirement (Non-Qualified)

                [ ] Other _____

Owner Name(s) on Account _____

Name of Annuitant(s) _____

Value of Annuity $_____, as of date _____/_____/_____

Authorized Signers on Account   _____

Statement Mailing Address   _____

                            _____

Online Banking Username   _____

Online Banking Password   _____

[ ] Release on File

Company Name _____

    Account/Contract Number _____

    Location of Original Annuity Contract _____

    Company Address _____

    Company Phone Number _____

Type of Account   [ ] Deferred   [ ] Immediate

                [ ] IRA/401(k)/Retirement (Qualified)

                [ ] Non-Retirement (Non-Qualified)

                [ ] Other _____

Owner Name(s) on Account _____

Name of Annuitant(s) _____

Value of Annuity $_____, as of date _____/_____/_____

Authorized Signers on Account   _____

Statement Mailing Address   _____

                            _____

Online Banking Username   _____

Online Banking Password   _____

[ ] Release on File

Life Insurance

Company Name _____

    Account/Policy Number _____

    Location of Original Insurance Policy _____

    Company Address _____

    Company Phone Number _____

Type of Insurance   [ ] Term   [ ] Whole Life

                  [ ] Other _____

Owner Name(s) on Account _____

Name of Insured Person(s) _____

Policy Beneficiary _____

Face Value of Policy $_____

Cash Value of Policy $_____, as of date _____/_____/_____

Authorized Signers on Account   _____

Statement Mailing Address   _____

                              _____

Online Banking Username   _____

Online Banking Password   _____

[ ] Release on File

Company Name _____

    Account/Policy Number _____

    Location of Original Insurance Policy _____

    Company Address _____

    Company Phone Number _____

Type of Insurance   [ ] Term   [ ] Whole Life

                  [ ] Other _____

Owner Name(s) on Account _____

Name of Insured Person(s) _____

Policy Beneficiary _____

Face Value of Policy $_____

Cash Value of Policy $_____, as of date _____/_____/_____

Authorized Signers on Account   _____

Statement Mailing Address   _____

                              _____

Online Banking Username   _____

Online Banking Password   _____

[ ] Release on File

Company Name _____

    Account/Policy Number _____

    Location of Original Insurance Policy _____

    Company Address_____

    Company Phone Number _____

Type of Insurance [ ] Term   [ ] Whole Life

                [ ] Other _____

Owner Name(s) on Account _____

Name of Insured Person(s) _____

Policy Beneficiary _____

Face Value of Policy $_____

Cash Value of Policy $_____, as of date _____/_____/_____

Authorized Signers on Account   _____

Statement Mailing Address   _____

                                      _____

Online Banking Username   _____

Online Banking Password   _____

[ ] Release on File

Company Name _____

    Account/Policy Number _____

    Location of Original Insurance Policy _____

    Company Address_____

    Company Phone Number _____

Type of Insurance [ ] Term   [ ] Whole Life

                [ ] Other _____

Owner Name(s) on Account _____

Name of Insured Person(s) _____

Policy Beneficiary _____

Face Value of Policy $_____

Cash Value of Policy $_____, as of date _____/_____/_____

Authorized Signers on Account   _____

Statement Mailing Address   _____

                                        _____

Online Banking Username   _____

Online Banking Password   _____

[ ] Release on File

Cars/Automobiles/Vehicles

Year/Make/Model _____

License Plate Number _____ State of Registration _____

Vehicle Identification Number/VIN _____

Owner on Title/Loan _____

Vehicle Loan/Lease Lender _____

    Bank Address _____

    Bank Phone Number _____ Loan Account Number _____

    [ ] Release on File

Location of Vehicle _____

Location of Pink Slip _____

Year/Make/Model _____

License Plate Number _____ State of Registration _____

Vehicle Identification Number/VIN _____

Owner on Title/Loan _____

Vehicle Loan/Lease Lender _____

    Bank Address _____

    Bank Phone Number _____ Loan Account Number _____

    [ ] Release on File

Location of Vehicle _____

Location of Pink Slip _____

Year/Make/Model _____

License Plate Number _____ State of Registration _____

Vehicle Identification Number/VIN _____

Owner on Title/Loan _____

Vehicle Loan/Lease Lender _____

    Bank Address _____

    Bank Phone Number _____ Loan Account Number _____

    [ ] Release on File

Location of Vehicle _____

Location of Pink Slip _____

Year/Make/Model _____

License Plate Number _____ State of Registration _____

Vehicle Identification Number/VIN _____

Owner on Title/Loan _____

Vehicle Loan/Lease Lender _____

    Bank Address _____

    Bank Phone Number _____ Loan Account Number _____

    [ ] Release on File

Location of Vehicle _____

Location of Pink Slip _____

Year/Make/Model _____

License Plate Number _____ State of Registration _____

Vehicle Identification Number/VIN _____

Owner on Title/Loan _____

Vehicle Loan/Lease Lender _____

    Bank Address _____

    Bank Phone Number _____ Loan Account Number _____

    [ ] Release on File

Location of Vehicle _____

Location of Pink Slip _____

Year/Make/Model _____

License Plate Number _____ State of Registration _____

Vehicle Identification Number/VIN _____

Owner on Title/Loan _____

Vehicle Loan/Lease Lender _____

    Bank Address _____

    Bank Phone Number _____ Loan Account Number _____

    [ ] Release on File

Location of Vehicle _____

Location of Pink Slip _____

Year/Make/Model _____

License Plate Number _____ State of Registration _____

Vehicle Identification Number/VIN _____

Owner on Title/Loan _____

Vehicle Loan/Lease Lender _____

    Bank Address _____

    Bank Phone Number _____ Loan Account Number _____

    [ ] Release on File

Location of Vehicle _____

Location of Pink Slip _____

Year/Make/Model _____

License Plate Number _____ State of Registration _____

Vehicle Identification Number/VIN _____

Owner on Title/Loan _____

Vehicle Loan/Lease Lender _____

    Bank Address _____

    Bank Phone Number _____ Loan Account Number _____

    [ ] Release on File

Location of Vehicle _____

Location of Pink Slip _____

Year/Make/Model _____

License Plate Number _____ State of Registration _____

Vehicle Identification Number/VIN _____

Owner on Title/Loan _____

Vehicle Loan/Lease Lender _____

    Bank Address _____

    Bank Phone Number _____ Loan Account Number _____

    [ ] Release on File

Location of Vehicle _____

Location of Pink Slip _____

Other Debts

Creditor/Bank Name _____

    Account Number _____

    Bank Address _____

    Bank Phone Number _____

Type of Debt   [ ] Credit Card   [ ] Line of Credit   [ ] Promissory Note

                [ ] Equity Line   [ ] Auto Loan   [ ] Business Line

                [ ] Business Credit Card [ ] Other _____

Name(s) on Account _____

Amount of Credit/Loan Line $_____   Average Balance Owed $_____

Regular Payment Amount $_____, monthly/quarterly/annually

Regular Payment Due Date _____ on the _____ of each month

Interest Rate _____ % APR   Automatic Payment: [ ] yes   [ ] no

Authorized Signer(s) on Account _____

Statement Mailing Address _____

Credit Card Number _____

    Card PIN _____ Card Expiration Date _____/_____/_____

    CCV Code/Code on Back of Card _____

Online Banking Username _____

Online Banking Password _____

[ ] Release on File

* * * *

Creditor/Bank Name _____

    Account Number _____

    Bank Address _____

    Bank Phone Number _____

Type of Debt   [ ] Credit Card   [ ] Line of Credit   [ ] Promissory Note

                [ ] Equity Line   [ ] Auto Loan   [ ] Business Line

                [ ] Business Credit Card [ ] Other _____

Name(s) on Account _____

Amount of Credit/Loan Line $_____   Average Balance Owed $_____

Regular Payment Amount $_____, monthly/quarterly/annually

Regular Payment Due Date _____ on the _____ of each month

Interest Rate _____ % APR   Automatic Payment: [ ] yes   [ ] no

Authorized Signer(s) on Account _____

Statement Mailing Address _____

Credit Card Number _____

Card PIN _____ Card Expiration Date _____/_____/_____

CCV Code/Code on Back of Card _____

Online Banking Username _____

Online Banking Password _____

[ ] Release on File

* * * *

Creditor/Bank Name _____

    Account Number _____

    Bank Address _____

    Bank Phone Number _____

Type of Debt   [ ] Credit Card   [ ] Line of Credit   [ ] Promissory Note

               [ ] Equity Line   [ ] Auto Loan   [ ] Business Line

               [ ] Business Credit Card [ ] Other _____

Name(s) on Account _____

Amount of Credit/Loan Line $_____   Average Balance Owed $_____

Regular Payment Amount $_____, monthly/quarterly/annually

Regular Payment Due Date _____ on the _____ of each month

Interest Rate _____ % APR   Automatic Payment: [ ] yes   [ ] no

Authorized Signer(s) on Account _____

Statement Mailing Address _____

Credit Card Number _____

    Card PIN _____ Card Expiration Date _____/_____/_____

    CCV Code/Code on Back of Card _____

Online Banking Username _____

Online Banking Password _____

[ ] Release on File

* * * *

Creditor/Bank Name _____

    Account Number _____

    Bank Address _____

    Bank Phone Number _____

Type of Debt   [ ] Credit Card   [ ] Line of Credit   [ ] Promissory Note

               [ ] Equity Line   [ ] Auto Loan   [ ] Business Line

               [ ] Business Credit Card [ ] Other _____

Name(s) on Account _____

Amount of Credit/Loan Line $_____   Average Balance Owed $_____

Regular Payment Amount $_____, monthly/quarterly/annually

Regular Payment Due Date _____ on the _____ of each month

Interest Rate _____ % APR   Automatic Payment: [ ] yes   [ ] no

Authorized Signer(s) on Account _____

Statement Mailing Address _____

Credit Card Number _____

    Card PIN _____ Card Expiration Date _____/_____/_____

    CCV Code/Code on Back of Card _____

Online Banking Username _____

Online Banking Password _____

[ ] Release on File

* * * *

Creditor/Bank Name _____

    Account Number _____

    Bank Address _____

    Bank Phone Number _____

Type of Debt   [ ] Credit Card   [ ] Line of Credit   [ ] Promissory Note

                 [ ] Equity Line   [ ] Auto Loan   [ ] Business Line

                 [ ] Business Credit Card   [ ] Other _____

Name(s) on Account _____

Amount of Credit/Loan Line $_____   Average Balance Owed $_____

Regular Payment Amount $_____, monthly/quarterly/annually

Regular Payment Due Date _____ on the _____ of each month

Interest Rate _____ % APR   Automatic Payment: [ ] yes   [ ] no

Authorized Signer(s) on Account _____

Statement Mailing Address _____

Credit Card Number _____

    Card PIN _____ Card Expiration Date _____/_____/_____

    CCV Code/Code on Back of Card _____

Online Banking Username _____

Online Banking Password _____

[ ] Release on File

* * * *

Income

Source of Income	Husband (annual)	Wife (annual)
Social Security	$	$
Social Security	$	$
Pension (Source _____)	$	$
Pension (Source _____)	$	$
Pension (Source _____)	$	$
Pension (Source _____)	$	$
Pension (Source _____)	$	$
Pension (Source _____)	$	$
IRA/401(k)/Retirement (Source _____)	$	$
IRA/401(k)/Retirement (Source _____)	$	$
IRA/401(k)/Retirement (Source _____)	$	$
IRA/401(k)/Retirement (Source _____)	$	$
IRA/401(k)/Retirement (Source _____)	$	$
Rental Income/Real Estate (Source _____)	$	$
Rental Income/Real Estate (Source _____)	$	$
Rental Income/Real Estate (Source _____)	$	$
Investment Income (Source _____)	$	$
Investment Income (Source _____)	$	$
Investment Income (Source _____)	$	$
Investment Income (Source _____)	$	$
Investment Income (Source _____)	$	$
Other (Source _____)	$	$
Other (Source _____)	$	$
Other (Source _____)	$	$

Home Safe(s)

Location in Home _____

Who Has Access _____

_____

Location of Key _____

Lock Combination _____

Contents _____

_____

_____

_____

Location in Home _____

Who Has Access _____

_____

Location of Key _____

Lock Combination _____

Contents _____

_____

_____

_____

Location in Home _____

Who Has Access _____

_____

Location of Key _____

Lock Combination _____

Contents _____

_____

_____

_____

Location in Home _____

Who Has Access _____

_____

Location of Key _____

Lock Combination _____

Contents _____

_____

_____

Safe Deposit Box(es)

Bank Name _____ Box Number _____

Box Number _____

Location of Key(s) _____

Branch Address _____

Branch Phone Number _____

Owner Name(s) on Box _____

Access Granted to _____

Bank Name _____ Box Number _____

Box Number _____

Location of Key(s) _____

Branch Address _____

Branch Phone Number _____

Owner Name(s) on Box _____

Access Granted to _____

Bank Name _____ Box Number _____

Box Number _____

Location of Key(s) _____

Branch Address _____

Branch Phone Number _____

Owner Name(s) on Box _____

Access Granted to _____

Notes:

_____

_____

_____

_____

_____

_____

_____

_____

_____

_____

Notes:

Notes:

_____

_____

_____

_____

_____

_____

_____

_____

_____

_____

_____

_____

_____

_____

_____

_____

_____

_____

_____

_____

_____

_____

_____

_____

_____

_____

_____

_____

_____

Notes:

Chapter 10

ESTATE PLAN

My Story:

"My dad was in a memory care unit for a little while. It was not uncommon for residents to steal things from forks to sugar packs. My dad loved to steal jigsaw puzzle pieces and put them in the basket under his walker seat. So at every visit we would search his room and return the puzzle pieces to their original places. Oh by the way, we also found and returned the sugar packets, movies, CDs from the common area, candies, other resident's clothes, and more. He became a real kleptomaniac. But, the other residents took his stuff also, so I guess it works out in the long run!"

Living Trust

    Name/Title of Trust _____

    Date Trust First Signed _____

    Date of First Amendment/Restatement _____

    Date of Second Amendment/Restatement _____

    Date of Third Amendment/Restatement _____

    Date of Fourth Amendment/Restatement _____

    Name of Primary/Initial Trustee(s)* _____

        Currently Serving as Trustee? (yes/no) _____ Co-Trustee? (yes/no) _____

    Name of Primary/Initial Trustee(s)* _____

        Currently Serving as Trustee? (yes/no) _____ Co-Trustee? (yes/no) _____

    Successor Trustee(s) _____

        Currently Serving as Trustee? (yes/no) _____ Co-Trustee? (yes/no) _____

    Successor Trustee(s) _____

        Currently Serving as Trustee? (yes/no) _____ Co-Trustee? (yes/no) _____

    Successor Trustee(s) _____

        Currently Serving as Trustee? (yes/no) _____ Co-Trustee? (yes/no) _____

    Location of Document _____

* this is usually the creator of the trust

Name/Title of Trust _____

Date Trust First Signed _____

Date of First Amendment/Restatement _____

Date of Second Amendment/Restatement _____

Date of Third Amendment/Restatement _____

Date of Fourth Amendment/Restatement _____

Name of Primary/Initial Trustee(s) _____

    Currently Serving as Trustee? (yes/no) _____ Co-Trustee? (yes/no) _____

Name of Primary/Initial Trustee(s) _____

    Currently Serving as Trustee? (yes/no) _____ Co-Trustee? (yes/no) _____

Successor Trustee(s) _____

    Currently Serving as Trustee? (yes/no) _____ Co-Trustee? (yes/no) _____

Successor Trustee(s) _____

    Currently Serving as Trustee? (yes/no) _____ Co-Trustee? (yes/no) _____

Successor Trustee(s) _____

    Currently Serving as Trustee? (yes/no) _____ Co-Trustee? (yes/no) _____

Type of Trust (if applicable) _____

Location of Document _____

Last Will/Last Will & Testament

Date Will First Signed _____

Date of First Codicil _____

Date of Second Codicil _____

Date of Third Codicil _____

Date of Fourth Codicil _____

First Named Executor(s) _____

    Co-Executor? (yes/no) _____

Successor Executor(s) _____

    Co-Executor? (yes/no) _____

Successor Executor(s) _____

    Co-Executor? (yes/no) _____

Successor Executor(s) _____

    Co-Executor? (yes/no) _____

Location of Document _____

Power of Attorney (POA)

First Named Agent(s) _____

Co-Agent? (yes/no) _____

Successor Agent(s) _____

Co-Agent? (yes/no) _____

Successor Agent(s) _____

Co-Agent? (yes/no) _____

Successor Agent(s) _____

Co-Agent? (yes/no) _____

Location of Document _____

Type of Document (check all that apply)*

[ ] Current POA   [ ] Durable POA

[ ] Not Durable POA   [ ] Springing POA (threshold satisfied)

[ ] Springing POA (threshold not satisfied)

Health Care Advance Directive

First Named Agent(s) _____

Co-Agent? (yes/no) _____

Successor Agent(s) _____

Co-Agent? (yes/no) _____

Successor Agent(s) _____

Co-Agent? (yes/no) _____

Successor Agent(s) _____

Co-Agent? (yes/no) _____

Location of Document _____

HIPAA Release

Authorized Persons Under HIPAA (list names)

_____   _____

_____   _____

_____   _____

Location of Document _____

POLST Document

Location of Document _____

Darte Document Signed _____

* see "Releases" section and glossary for more information about the types of powers of attorney

<u>Trustee/Executor/Agent Contact Information</u>

1)   Name _____

       Address _____

       _____

       Phone Number _____ Cell Phone Number _____

       Fax Number _____ Email _____

       To Act As   [ ] Trustee   [ ] Executor [ ] POA Agent   [ ] Health Care Agent

       Currently acting as Trustee/Executor/Agent?   [ ] yes   [ ] no

2)   Name _____

       Address _____

       _____

       Phone Number _____ Cell Phone Number _____

       Fax Number _____ Email _____

       To Act As   [ ] Trustee   [ ] Executor [ ] POA Agent   [ ] Health Care Agent

       Currently acting as Trustee/Executor/Agent?   [ ] yes   [ ] no

3)   Name _____

       Address _____

       _____

       Phone Number _____ Cell Phone Number _____

       Fax Number _____ Email _____

       To Act As   [ ] Trustee   [ ] Executor [ ] POA Agent   [ ] Health Care Agent

       Currently acting as Trustee/Executor/Agent?   [ ] yes   [ ] no

4)   Name _____

       Address _____

       _____

       Phone Number _____ Cell Phone Number _____

       Fax Number _____ Email _____

       To Act As   [ ] Trustee   [ ] Executor [ ] POA Agent   [ ] Health Care Agent

       Currently acting as Trustee/Executor/Agent?   [ ] yes   [ ] no

5)   Name _____

       Address _____

       _____

Phone Number _____ Cell Phone Number _____
Fax Number _____ Email _____
To Act As   [ ] Trustee   [ ] Executor [ ] POA Agent   [ ] Health Care Agent
Currently acting as Trustee/Executor/Agent?   [ ] yes   [ ] no

6)   Name _____
       Address _____

       _____

       Phone Number _____ Cell Phone Number _____
       Fax Number _____ Email _____
       To Act As   [ ] Trustee   [ ] Executor [ ] POA Agent   [ ] Health Care Agent
       Currently acting as Trustee/Executor/Agent?   [ ] yes   [ ] no

7)   Name _____
       Address _____

       _____

       Phone Number _____ Cell Phone Number _____
       Fax Number _____ Email _____
       To Act As   [ ] Trustee   [ ] Executor [ ] POA Agent   [ ] Health Care Agent
       Currently acting as Trustee/Executor/Agent?   [ ] yes   [ ] no

8)   Name _____
       Address _____

       _____

       Phone Number _____ Cell Phone Number _____
       Fax Number _____ Email _____
       To Act As   [ ] Trustee   [ ] Executor [ ] POA Agent   [ ] Health Care Agent
       Currently acting as Trustee/Executor/Agent?   [ ] yes   [ ] no

9)   Name _____
       Address _____

       _____

       Phone Number _____ Cell Phone Number _____
       Fax Number _____ Email _____
       To Act As   [ ] Trustee   [ ] Executor [ ] POA Agent   [ ] Health Care Agent
       Currently acting as Trustee/Executor/Agent?   [ ] yes   [ ] no

Notes:

Notes:

Chapter 11

SERVICE PROVIDERS

My Story:

"There are two things that are important to seniors that need care….food and TV. Disruption of either is an act of war! As you know the remote controls used for the TV can be quite daunting and if a wrong button is pushed, and the TV goes out, the cries for help begin immediately! Trying to navigate through the remote control buttons on the phone is very difficult and often times the TV problem compounds as multiple buttons have been pushed. So, of course, usually at 9PM or later, my wife and I would have to travel down to my mother-in-laws' assisted living (30 minutes each way) to fix the TV picture. After a few times doing this, I figured that there has to be a better way. I took a picture of her remote control and could then navigate her through the fix by phone…voila…about 30 hours saved that year!"

Phone/Internet/Television

Phone Lines:

Service   [ ] Main   [ ] Cell   [ ] Fax

Company Name _____ Phone Number _____

Address _____

Account Number _____ Auto Pay? yes _____ no _____

Auto Pay From Which Account? _____

Customer Service Username _____ Password _____

Customer Service Security PIN/Other Notes _____

Release on File? [ ]

Service   [ ] Main   [ ] Cell   [ ] Fax

Company Name _____ Phone Number _____

Address _____

Account Number _____ Auto Pay? yes _____ no _____

Auto Pay From Which Account? _____

Customer Service Username _____ Password _____

Customer Service Security PIN/Other Notes _____

Release on File? [ ]

Service   [ ] Main   [ ] Cell   [ ] Fax

Company Name _____ Phone Number _____

Address _____

Account Number _____ Auto Pay? yes _____ no _____

Auto Pay From Which Account? _____

Customer Service Username _____ Password _____

Customer Service Security PIN/Other Notes _____

Release on File? [ ]

Phone Voicemail Access

     Service   [ ] Main   [ ] Cell   [ ] Fax
     Access Number _____ PIN _____
     Notes _____

     _____

     Service   [ ] Main   [ ] Cell   [ ] Fax
     Access Number _____ PIN _____
     Notes _____

     _____

Television:

     Company Name _____ Phone Number _____
     Address _____
     Account Number _____ Auto Pay? yes ____ no ____
     Auto Pay From Which Account? _____
     Customer Service Username _____ Password _____
     Customer Service Security PIN/Other Notes _____
     Release on File? [ ]

Television Subscription Services (Internet TV, movies, etc.):

     Company Name _____ Phone Number _____
     Account Number _____ Auto Pay? yes ____ no ____
     Auto Pay From Which Account? _____
     Customer Service Username _____ Password _____
     Customer Service Security PIN/Other Notes _____
     Release on File? [ ]

     Company Name _____ Phone Number _____
     Account Number _____ Auto Pay? yes ____ no ____
     Auto Pay From Which Account? _____
     Customer Service Username _____ Password _____
     Customer Service Security PIN/Other Notes _____
     Release on File? [ ]

Utilities/Other Services

Internet:

Company Name _____ Phone Number _____

Address _____

Account Number _____ Auto Pay? yes _____ no _____

Auto Pay From Which Account? _____

Computer Access Username _____ Password _____

Wifi Network Name _____ Password _____

Customer Service Username _____ Password _____

Customer Service Security PIN/Other Notes _____

Release on File? [ ]

Electricity:

Company Name _____ Phone Number _____

Address _____

Account Number _____ Auto Pay? yes _____ no _____

Auto Pay From Which Account? _____

Release on File? [ ]

Gas/Propane/Heating Oil:

Company Name _____ Phone Number _____

Address _____

Account Number _____ Auto Pay? yes _____ no _____

Auto Pay From Which Account? _____

Release on File? [ ]

Company Name _____ Phone Number _____

Address _____

Account Number _____ Auto Pay? yes _____ no _____

Auto Pay From Which Account? _____

Release on File? [ ]

Water:

    Company Name _____ Phone Number _____

    Address _____

    Account Number _____ Auto Pay? yes _____ no _____

    Auto Pay From Which Account? _____

    Release on File? [ ]

Home Security System:

    Company Name _____ Phone Number _____

    Address _____

    Emergency Phone Number _____ System PIN/Password _____

    Account Number _____ Auto Pay? yes _____ no _____

    Auto Pay From Which Account? _____

    Notes on Security System/Alarm _____

    _____

    Release on File? [ ]

Identity Theft Protection Service:

    Company Name _____ Phone Number _____

    Address _____

    Account Number _____ Auto Pay? yes _____ no _____

    Auto Pay From Which Account? _____

    Customer Service Username _____ Password _____

    Customer Service Security PIN/Other Notes _____

    Release on File? [ ]

Pest Control:

    Company Name _____ Phone Number _____

    Address _____

    Account Number _____ Auto Pay? yes _____ no _____

    Auto Pay From Which Account? _____

    Frequency of Service/Service Schedule _____

    Release on File? [ ]

Gardener/Landscaping/Swimming Pool Service #1:

    Type of Service _____

    Company Name _____ Phone Number _____

    Address _____

    Account Number _____ Auto Pay? yes _____ no _____

    Auto Pay From Which Account? _____

    Frequency of Service/Service Schedule _____

    Release on File? [ ]

Gardener/Landscaping/Swimming Pool Service #2:

    Type of Service _____

    Company Name _____ Phone Number _____

    Address _____

    Account Number _____ Auto Pay? yes _____ no _____

    Auto Pay From Which Account? _____

    Frequency of Service/Service Schedule _____

    Release on File? [ ]

Subscriptions:

    Type of Service _____

    Company Name _____ Phone Number _____

    Account Number _____ Auto Pay? yes _____ no _____

    Auto Pay From Which Account? _____

    Customer Service Username _____ Password _____

    Address Publication Sent To _____

    Release on File? [ ]

    Type of Service _____

    Company Name _____ Phone Number _____

    Account Number _____ Auto Pay? yes _____ no _____

    Auto Pay From Which Account? _____

    Customer Service Username _____ Password _____

    Address Publication Sent To _____

    Release on File? [ ]

Storage Units:

    Company Name _____ Phone Number _____

    Account Number _____ Auto Pay? yes _____ no _____

    Auto Pay From Which Account? _____

    Customer Service Username _____ Password _____

    Unit Number _____ Lock / Combination_____

    Important Contents _____

    _____

    _____

    Release on File? [ ]

Other Service Providers:

    Type of Service _____

    Company Name _____ Phone Number _____

    Account Number _____ Auto Pay? yes _____ no _____

    Auto Pay From Which Account? _____

    Customer Service Username _____ Password _____

    Release on File? [ ]

    Type of Service _____

Company Name _____ Phone Number _____

    Account Number _____ Auto Pay? yes _____ no _____

    Auto Pay From Which Account? _____

    Customer Service Username _____ Password _____

    Release on File? [ ]

    Type of Service _____

    Company Name _____ Phone Number _____

    Account Number _____ Auto Pay? yes _____ no _____

    Auto Pay From Which Account? _____

    Customer Service Username _____ Password _____

    Release on File? [ ]

Notes:

Notes:

Notes:

_____

_____

_____

_____

_____

_____

_____

_____

_____

_____

_____

_____

_____

_____

_____

_____

_____

_____

_____

_____

_____

_____

_____

_____

_____

_____

_____

_____

_____

_____

_____

Chapter 12

OTHER HELPFUL RESOURCES & INFORMATION

A Friend's Story:

"If you are caring for an elderly person, you may have experienced what I call their "second childhood". Many seniors, my grandfather included, seem to become more childlike as they age, particularly in their later years, especially if they are coping with memory problems. For example, my grandfather sometimes went back to the good old days of playing cowboys and Indians when he got into his mid-80's (the dementia certainly was a factor!). He was always very proud of his genuine Stetson hat, and he took to wearing it around his assisted living villa a bit more often as the days went by. He even used to patrol the halls of the memory care wing looking for the "bad guys" in the black cowboy hats (his hat was white, so he was one of the "good guys"), and I am sure I heard him talking about the O.K. Corral a few times too... What mattered was that he always had a smile on his face when he was taking on his duties as sheriff of the memory care home, and the staff were kind enough to indulge him. Maybe you have experienced this too with your family members. I hope you have similar funny memories, which can help to brighten up the challenges of caring for an aging loved one."

Safety Checklist

The two most common causes of trips to the hospital are falls and medication errors. Taking reasonable steps to prevent a fall or overdose (or an under dose) can save a lot of anguish and possibly the elder's life.

Regardless of where your elder lives, it is useful to conduct your own fall risk assessment at the elder's residence. It may even help if you use a walker to mimic the actions and movements that the elder will take. "Being the elder" engulfs you in the scene. It is amazing what you can miss by not putting yourself in the shoes of the elder.

The below checklist is fairly comprehensive but should not be considered all inclusive, as each living situation is different. This list is designed to point out potential hazards but determining what corrective action is needed is up to the reader based on the specific issue being addressed.

* * * *

Common Safety Concerns for the Entire Residence	Deficient	OK	Notes
Smoke detectors			
CO$_2$ detectors			
Adequate regular lighting throughout the living space			
Night lighting of light switches throughout the living space			
Removal of clutter and clear walking pathways			
Able to navigate entire home with walker if needed			
Windows can easily open and close			
Fire extinguisher available in appropriate locations			
Space heaters are safe and placed away from fire hazards			
Floor "lip" or "threshold" trip hazards eliminated			
Possible slippery areas (when wet) eliminated			
Adequate clearances under all hanging items			
Adequate safety and security system			
General Personal Safety Concerns	**Deficient**	**OK**	**Notes**
Walker in good repair			
All shoes provide good and stable support			
Adequate medicine management in place (self/facility/family)			
Specific and dedicated area for medicine/medicine easily accessible			
Regular training on all emergency and non-emergency systems			
911 emergency systems			
Emergency buttons			
Fire extinguishers			

THE ELDERCARE READY PACK 165

General Personal Safety Concerns (continued)	Deficient	OK	Notes
Stove and microwave			
TV			
Phone			
Security system, if any			
Medicine management, if self administered			
Bathrooms	**Deficient**	**OK**	**Notes**
Path into bathroom well lit			
Toilet seat raised adequately			
Grab bars			
Around toilet			
In shower			
Near bathtub			
Bathmats in bathroom			
Nonslip backing			
Not curling up on edges or edges curled under			
Soap accessible without reaching			
Shower			
Tub			
Sink			
Soap residue removed regularly (to avoid slippery surfaces)			
Shower includes nonskid mat, decals, or strips			
Tub includes nonskid mat, decals, or strips			

Bathrooms (continued)	Deficient	OK	Notes
Towel rack easily accessible without reaching			
Shower chair installed, if needed			
Tub transfer bench installed, if needed			
Hand held shower wand installed, if needed			
Bathtub height is appropriate for easy entry and exit			
Shower or bath water does not get too hot			
Hot and cold faucets are clearly marked			
Shower curtain is secure or bolted to the wall			
Shower stall has shatterproof glass (if applicable)			
Medications kept in bathroom are easily accessible (if applicable)			
All toiletries are easily accessible			
Lights are easily accessible			
Light switches are clearly marked			
Night lighting is adequate			

Bedroom(s)	Deficient	OK	Notes
Night table is available and accessible from bed			
Night table includes lamp and glasses holder (if needed)			
Lamp switch is easily accessible			
Phone is within reach of bed			
Flashlight is easily accessible			
Cords in room are not a trip/fall hazard			
Floor is not cluttered			

Bedroom(s) (continued)	Deficient	OK	Notes
Night lights are available (preferably motion sensor lights)			
Night lights light path to bathroom			
Wall light switches are easily accessible even in the dark			
Bed is at correct height for ease of entry and exit			
Furniture is not a trip/fall hazard and permits ease of movement			
Pathways are clear			
If carpeted, throw rugs are removed (to reduce trip hazards)			
Existing rugs are secure with no fraying or edges curled			
Furniture is able to offer support if needed			
Dresser drawers are easy to open and close			
Bed rails or assist handles are installed (if needed)			
Easy access in and out of bed			
Emergency alert system (if available) is accessible from bed			
Bedside commode is accessible (if needed)			
Adequate heating and cooling are provided			
Adequate bedding is provided			
Kitchen	**Deficient**	**OK**	**Notes**
Throw rugs/floor mats are secure with no curling edges			
All kitchen items are easily accessible			
All food items are easily accessible			
Microwave is easily accessible			
Flooring is not slippery (in general)			

Kitchen (continued)	Deficient	OK	Notes
Light switches are easily accessible (even in dark)			
Stove controls are easily located and understood			
Loose fitting towels, clothing, or curtains are safe from fire			
Cabinets are easily accessible (appropriate height)			
Counter tops are not cluttered			
Dangerous chemicals/cleaning materials are secure			
Chemicals are stored away from food			
Paper towels are not too close to the stove			
Other flammables are away from heat sources			
Sharp objects (knives, etc.) are secure			
Sturdy step stool, if needed, is available and has handrail(s)			
General Living Areas	**Deficient**	**OK**	**Notes**
Floor coverings are nonskid			
Phone is easily accessible from common resting areas			
All cords are hidden/not a trip hazard			
Light switches are easily accessible (even in dark)			
Emergency alarm device is accessible from all sitting areas			
Furniture placement is easy to navigate			
Ceiling fan switches are easily accessible (if available)			
Handrails are available on both sides of the stairs (if applicable)			
Handrails are firmly attached to their supports			
Steps are all even and safe			

General Living Areas (continued)	Deficient	OK	Notes
Full lighting is available on all stair areas			
Top and bottom stairs are clearly marked			
Chairs are not on rollers, if possible			
Chairs are secure (not wobbly)			
Sliding chairs are secure			
Chairs or sofa are easy to enter/exit (swiveling, if available)			
Seating areas are easily accessible			
Throw rugs and carpet runners are removed or well secured			
Carpet is in good shape (not torn or frayed)			
Non-carpeted areas are non-skid/not slippery			
Tables are secure and stable			
Glare from windows is not too bright			
Miscellaneous	**Deficient**	**OK**	**Notes**
Laundry Areas			
Detergent is easy to lift and pour/scoop			
Laundry baskets are not too large or heavy			
Garage			
Stairs are well lit and easy to navigate			
Garage is not too cluttered			
Tools and other machinery are secure			
Garage is secure (from outside)			
Exterior of Residence			

Miscellaneous (continued)	Deficient	OK	Notes
Driveway is not too steep, cracked, or uneven			
Driveway is free of snow and ice hazards			
Adequate lighting is provided in all travel areas			
Doorbell is loud enough to hear			
Handrails are provided for steps to door, if possible			
Pathways are clear of leaves and debris			
All doors are easily accessible			
Ramp, if needed, is secure			
Pets			
Sleeping areas for pets are out of traffic areas			
Pet food and bowls are easily accessible			
Pet's items do not pose trip/fall hazards			
General Security	**Deficient**	**OK**	**Notes**
Valuables			
Jewelry is secure			
Artwork/other valuables are secure			
Rental insurance is purchased and updated			
Locked closet area is available for valuables			

What to Do After the Death of a Loved One

Since many actions can affect the deceased elder's estate, including but not limited to, tax and other elections that may be beneficial in the administration of an estate, I suggest that, after a loved one's passing, no action other than the below be taken without the advice and counsel of an estate planning attorney.

As soon as possible:

1. Determine whether any of decedent's property needs to be safeguarded, such as a motor vehicle, vacant residence or rental house, and the like. Secure property from potential loss such as theft and vandalism.

2. Ensure that proper funeral arrangements have been made and carried out per the wishes of the elder. The funeral home should order death certificates, and normally six to twelve of them are sufficient. For larger estates, one certificate per deed or financial account may be needed.

3. Contact an estate planning attorney such as myself immediately and engage the firm for legal services relating to settlement and administration of the trust and/or estate. If the elder does not have an estate planning attorney, please feel free to contact my office for a possible referral. I can be reached by email at sfurman@socallegalcenter.com or by phone (toll free) at (877) 820-3335.

4. Take possession of the original living trust and last will documents. Do not write on original documents.

5. Meet with the attorney and follow his/her instructions.

6. Bring your *ElderCare Ready Book* or *ElderCare Ready Pack* information and documentation to the consultation. The attorney will be very impressed, and it will save you attorney's fees!

* * * *

Journal

Use this section to add notes for any important miscellaneous information that you may want to write down. This could be important conversations that you had with the elder or a family member, or just information that you want to keep track of for any reason.

* * * *

Date: _____

Notes:_____

_____

_____

_____

Date: _____

Notes:_____

_____

_____

_____

Date: _____

Notes:_____

_____

_____

_____

Date: _____

Notes:_____

_____

_____

_____

Date: _____

Notes:_____

_____

_____

_____

Date: _____

Notes:_____

_____

_____

Date: _____

Notes:_____

_____

_____

_____

Date: _____

Notes:_____

_____

_____

_____

Date: _____

Notes:_____

_____

_____

_____

Date: _____

Notes:_____

_____

_____

_____

Date: _____

Notes:_____

_____

_____

_____

Date: _____

Notes:_____

_____

_____

_____

Date: _____

Notes:_____

_____

_____

_____

Date: _____

Notes:_____

_____

_____

_____

Date: _____

Notes:_____

_____

_____

_____

Date: _____

Notes:_____

_____

_____

_____

Date: _____

Notes:_____

_____

_____

_____

Date: _____

Notes:_____

_____

_____

_____

Date: _____

Notes:_____

_____

_____

_____

Date: _____

Notes:_____

_____

_____

_____

Date: _____

Notes:_____

_____

_____

_____

Date: _____

Notes:_____

_____

_____

_____

Date: _____

Notes:_____

_____

_____

_____

Date: _____

Notes:_____

_____

_____

_____

Date: _____

Notes:_____

_____

_____

_____

Date: _____

Notes:_____

_____

_____

_____

Date: _____

Notes:_____

_____

_____

_____

Notes:

Notes:

GLOSSARY OF TERMS & EXPLANATIONS

assessor's parcel number. The descriptive number assigned to real estate for tax assessment tracking purposes.

beneficiary. The person or organization entitled to the benefits of an estate, trust, life insurance policy, IRA, or other asset.

deferred annuity. An annuity contract where the funds compound tax deferred (meaning income tax is not paid on the earnings until they are withdrawn). These annuities are typically revocable and subject to paying a surrender charge for an early withdrawal. Surrender charges expire after a certain period as determined by the annuity contract.

estate planning. The planning for the transfer of assets upon death or for change in control if one is incapacitated.

health care advance directive. These are known by various other names across the country, including being called a "medical power of attorney." These documents grant the authority to another person to make medical decisions for you if you are unable to do so for yourself (due to legal incompetency or being sedated during surgery, etc.).

HIPAA release. A HIPAA release is similar to a general consent to release your medical information to the persons named in the HIPAA release.

hospice. A program paid through Medicare designed to assist people in the process of dying. All medicines designed to treat a person's illness are halted and only comfort medicines are provided to relieve pain. Hospice generally also provides counseling.

immediate annuity. An irrevocable annuity that pays a monthly amount to the annuitant (the person whose life the annuity is based upon) until the selected term expires or the annuitant dies.

impound account. Sometimes a lender on a home mortgage collects additional funds within the mortgage payment to pay the real estate taxes and insurance premiums and pays them when due. This account where that money is held is called an impound account.

irrevocable trust. A living trust that cannot be revoked, amended, or modified by the creator once signed.

living trust. An estate planning document executed to generally avoid probate and conservatorship (sometimes called guardianship for adults) proceedings. Assets are transferred to the named trustee, typically the creator of the trust, to be managed according to the trust provisions. In the event of the death or incapacity of the creator of the trust, the successor trustee takes over allowing for the smooth management transition.

long-term care insurance (LTCI). Insurance that provides benefits for stays in nursing homes, assisted living, and sometimes in independent living communities. The LTCI policy may also provide benefits for care at home. All policies are different. This is not a government program and is privately purchased.

Medicaid (Medi-Cal in California). A federal program implemented through the states; however, each state can and often does vary considerably on the implementation. California refers to its Medicaid program as Medi-Cal. Your state may also refer to Medicaid by a more generic name. The program provides financial support for long-term care in a nursing facility. Some states have programs to provide Medicaid benefits at the board-and-care level, and some programs provide benefits for care at home.

Medicare. The health insurance program for individuals available to those over the age of sixty-five. There are other health insurance programs under Medicare for disabled and other individuals that are not referred to in this book.

nonrecurring medications. Medications taken for a specific illness or issue and intended to be stopped once the illness is cured.

nonqualified accounts. Accounts that are not qualified accounts. These are also referred to as non-retirement accounts. See "qualified accounts" on the following page.

pour-over will. A will that names the creator's living trust as the beneficiary.

power of attorney. A document authorizing a person to act on behalf of another according to the terms of the document.

current durable power of attorney. A durable power of attorney that stays in effect after the principal (the one granting the power of attorney) has become legally incompetent.

springing durable power of attorney. A durable power of attorney that becomes effective ONLY after the principal (the one granting the power of attorney) has become legally incompetent. It "springs" into effect upon incapacity or when another condition is fulfilled which triggers the authority coming into effect. The threshold must be satisfied before the agent can use the power of attorney.

qualified account. A specific tax-deferred retirement account where no income taxes are paid on the income until it is withdrawn. The most common qualified accounts are IRAs and a 401(k). These are also referred to as retirement accounts.

recurring medications. Medications taken at prescribed intervals that are intended to continue indefinitely.

release on file. Please see detailed information on releases in the introductory section titled "Releases".

revocable trust. A living trust that can be revoked, amended, or modified by the creator.

RN or LVN. An RN is a registered nurse while an LVN is a licensed vocational nurse.

Rx name. The name of the medication.

settlor. The settlor is the creator of a living trust. The settlor may also be referred to as the trustor, grantor, transferor, creator, or trustmaker.

successor trustee. The individual or institution managing the trust if the initial trustee has died or is incapacitated.

skilled nursing home. Commonly known as a nursing home or convalescent home. Rehabilitation facilities sometimes come under this name.

testamentary trust. A trust created within a last will and testament.

trustee. The individual or institution who manages a trust.

veterans' benefits. A generic term to mean a pension paid to veterans meeting certain tests, and to their surviving spouses, to pay for costs of long-term care in an assisted living facility, board-and-care home, and for care at home. This is not referring to disability or compensation payments due to a service connected injury.

vesting. This is another word for whose name an asset is in. An account is "vested" in your name if your name appears on the account as opposed to an account that is in your living trust, in which case the account is vested in your living trust.

Notes:

Notes:

Notes:

About the Author

STUART FURMAN, ESQ.

STUART FURMAN HAS BEEN A member of the State Bar for the state of California and has been practicing law since 1981. He was accredited by the Department of Veterans Affairs as an accredited VA attorney in 2009. Mr. Furman's law practice has concentrated on elder law issues, including long-term care for seniors, planning for veterans and accessing VA benefits, Medi-Cal/Medicaid pre-planning and accessing Medi-Cal and Medicaid benefits, living trusts, wills, powers of attorney, advanced medical directives, and other peripheral issues.

Mr. Furman has educated nurses, discharge planners, and social workers in many Southern California hospitals. He has appeared as a guest on several radio programs in California. Mr. Furman has spoken for numerous organizations around California and has offered continuing education credits for real estate agents and brokers, board-and-care administrators, CPAs, EAs, and other professionals.

Mr. Furman is vice chair and sits on the board of directors of a large Visiting Nurses Association and hospice organization in Southern California. He is a member of the National Association of Elder Law Attorneys, ElderCounsel, the San Diego Society of Human Resource Management (SDSHRM), and is on the legislative committee for SDSHRM.

In his personal life, he has enjoyed his marriage to his wife Jayne for more than twenty-three years. He is an accomplished violinist, having begun the study of music at the age of nine. He has sat on the board of directors of several musical organizations and performed as a member of several professional orchestras across the United States.

Mr. Furman is available to speak about planning for eldercare, eldercare legal issues, long-term care planning, and general eldercare topics at your company HR department and to your employees, community center, assisted living community, radio or television program, or other appropriate venues or events.

Stuart Furman is also the owner of Southern California Legal Center, Inc. where he practices elder law with clients located throughout California. His law practice can be reached at (877) 820-3335 or by email at sfurman@socallegalcenter.com

CPSIA information can be obtained
at www.ICGtesting.com
Printed in the USA
FSOW04n0350200515
7165FS